# New Curriculum

# Primary English

Learn, practise and revise

Les Ray and Gill Budgell

Year **3**

# Contents

RISING STARS

# Content grid

## Links to English Programme of Study for Key Stage 2

| | Unit title | Objective | Focus | Speak about it |
|---|---|---|---|---|
| 1 | Tricky spelling | Use further prefixes and suffixes and understand how to add them; spell words that are often misspelt | Word reading, spelling and word structure | Terminology: prefix, suffix, root words |
| 2 | Building from root words | Apply their growing knowledge of root words, prefixes and suffixes | Word reading, spelling and word structure | Terminology: prefix, suffix, word families |
| 3 | Myths and legends | Increase familiarity with a wide range of books, including fairy stories, myths and legends; retell some myths and legends orally | Comprehension | Myths and legends, and building on own reading experiences |
| 4 | Headings and sub-headings | In non-narrative material, use simple organisational devices such as headings and sub-headings | Comprehension, composition and text structure | Terminology: headings and sub-headings<br><br>Usage and effect |
| 5 | Drawing Inferences: characters and feelings | Draw inferences such as inferring characters' feelings, thoughts and motives from their actions, and justifying inferences with evidence predicting what might happen from details stated and implied | Comprehension, composition and text structure | Characters and characterisation |
| 6 | Finding your way around reference texts | Retrieve and record information from non-fiction | Comprehension, composition and text structure | Terminology: reference, fiction, non-fiction |
| 7 | Test your grammar, punctuation and spelling | • Determiners<br>• Headings and sub-headings<br>• Capital letters, full stops, exclamation marks and question marks<br>• Adding the suffix -ly<br>• Exception words | | |
| 8 | Planning your writing: letters | Discuss writing similar to that which they are planning to write in order to understand and learn from its structure, grammar and vocabulary | Comprehension, composition and text structure | Purpose and audience |
| 9 | Planning your writing: instructions | Discuss writing similar to that which they are planning to write in order to understand and learn from its structure, grammar and vocabulary | Comprehension, composition and text structure | Features of instructional texts |
| 10 | Planning your writing: leaflets | Discuss writing similar to that which they are planning to write in order to understand and learn from its structure, grammar and vocabulary | Comprehension, composition and text structure | Features of information texts and persuasion |
| 11 | Suffixes with vowels | Add suffixes beginning with vowel letters to words of more than one syllable | Word reading, spelling and word structure | Terminology: suffix, vowels<br><br>Purpose and links to spelling and meaning |
| 12 | Prefixes | More prefixes | Word reading, spelling and word structure | Terminology: prefix<br><br>Purpose and links to spelling and meaning |
| 13 | Poems to perform | Prepare poems and playscripts to read aloud and to perform, showing understanding through intonation, tone, volume and action | Comprehension, composition and text structure | Verses, rhyme and patterns |

| | Unit title | Objective | Focus | Speak about it |
|---|---|---|---|---|
| 14 | Test your grammar, punctuation and spelling | • Using conjunctions to express time and cause<br>• Using adverbs to express time and cause<br>• Using commas in lists<br>• Word endings that sound like /zhun/<br>• Suffix -ous | | |
| 15 | Planning your writing: correct order, sequence | Organise paragraphs around a theme | Composition, sentence and text structure | Sequence and order |
| 16 | Planning your writing: problem solving | Organise paragraphs around a theme | Composition, sentence and text structure | Planning and techniques |
| 17 | Capturing imagination – words and phrases | Discuss words and phrases that capture the reader's interest and imagination | Word reading, spelling and word structure | Terminology: adjective and verb<br>Usage and purpose |
| 18 | Predicting what might happen | Draw inferences such as inferring characters' feelings, thoughts and motives from their actions, and justifying inferences with evidence predicting what might happen from details stated and implied | Comprehension, composition and text structure | Story endings |
| 19 | Time and place: drawing inferences | Draw inferences such as inferring characters' feelings, thoughts and motives from their actions, and justifying inferences with evidence predicting what might happen from details stated and implied | Comprehension, composition and text structure | Terminology: paragraph<br>Usage and purpose |
| 20 | Paragraphs 1 | Use paragraphs as a way to group related material | Comprehension, composition and text structure | Terminology: paragraph<br>Usage and purpose |
| 21 | Test your grammar, punctuation and spelling | • Using prepositions to express time and cause<br>• Word families<br>• Contractions<br>• Words with endings sounding like /zhuh/ or /chuh/<br>• Root words ending -tch or -ch plus -er | | |
| 22 | Paragraphs 2 | Use paragraphs as a way to group related material | Word reading, spelling and text structure | Terminology: paragraph, topic sentence<br>Usage and purpose |
| 23 | Punctuation of direct speech | Use and punctuate direct speech | Punctuation | Terminology: direct speech<br>Usage and purpose |
| 24 | Using connectives | Extend the range of sentences with more than one clause by using a wider range of conjunctions, e.g. *when, if, because, although* | Composition, sentence structure and text structure | Terminology: conjunctions<br>Usage and purpose |
| 25 | Clauses | Extend the range of sentences with more than one clause by using a wider range of conjunctions, e.g. *when, if, because, although* | Composition, sentence structure and punctuation | Terminology: clauses, phrases<br>Usage, purpose and effect |
| 26 | Choosing the best vocabulary and grammar – adjectives | Discuss writing similar to that which they are planning to write in order to understand and learn from its structure, grammar and vocabulary | Composition, word structure and sentence structure | Terminology: adjective<br>Usage, purpose and effect |
| 27 | Choosing the best vocabulary and grammar – verbs and adverbs | Discuss writing similar to that which they are planning to write in order to understand and learn from its structure, grammar and vocabulary | Composition, word structure and sentence structure | Terminology: verb, adverb, sentence<br>Usage, purpose and effect |
| 28 | Test your grammar, punctuation and spelling | • The perfect form of verbs<br>• Terminology: conjunction, adverb, preposition, prefix, consonant, vowel<br>• Inverted commas (speech marks)<br>• Adding prefixes<br>• Useful words | | |

# 1 Tricky spelling

Let's investigate how to spell words when you add prefixes and suffixes.
Each part of a word is like a building brick.

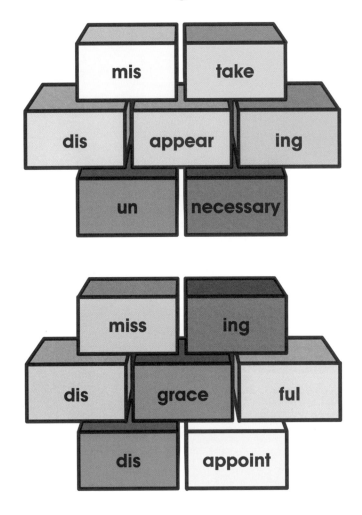

Look at how many new words we can make. We first have to find the
**root word**. These are **take**, **appear**, **necessary**, **miss**, **grace** and
**appoint**. Then we can add prefixes. These are **mis-**, **dis-** and **un-**.
We can sometimes also add suffixes such as **-ing** and **-ful**.

## Speak about it

Look at the pictures. How is a word 'like a building brick'?
What is a prefix?
What is a suffix?
Look at the way we build words on the page.
What are root words?

## Comprehension

1) Which root words are used in the examples?

2) Which prefixes are used in the examples?

3) Which prefixes make the word mean its opposite?

4) Which suffixes are used?

5) What are the new words we have made?

6) Does the spelling of the root word change in these examples when you add a prefix or a suffix?

## Language focus

1) Make these words mean something new by adding the prefixes **un-**, **mis-**, **dis-**, **in-** or **re-**.
   What happens to the spelling of the root word? Check your answers in a dictionary. Can you make a rule?

   **take     approve     definite     open     fresh     satisfied**

2) See if you can add the suffixes **-ly**, **-ment** or **-ing** to these words.
   What happens to the spelling of the root word? Check your answers in a dictionary. Can you make a rule?

   **definite     open     turn     slow     develop     excite**

3) Add **-ing** to these words ending in **-e**. What happens to the spelling? Check your answers in a dictionary. Can you make a rule?

   **complete     behave     replace     approve     hope**

## Links to writing

1) Make a list of other prefixes and suffixes. Experiment to see if you can build new words. Check your answers in a dictionary.

| Prefixes | Root words | Suffixes |
|---|---|---|
| dis-, un-, re-, in-, de- | place, appear, measure, charge, vent, grace, light | -ment, -ed, -ing, -able, -ful |

2) Write some 'handy hints' for a poster in your classroom to show people that there should not be a problem with spelling when you are adding prefixes and suffixes. Make sure you give some exceptions as well. Are there any words that double their last letter when you add a suffix, such as **begin** – **beginning**?

# 2 Building from root words

Look at the word-making machine.
See how you can build new words in the same family.

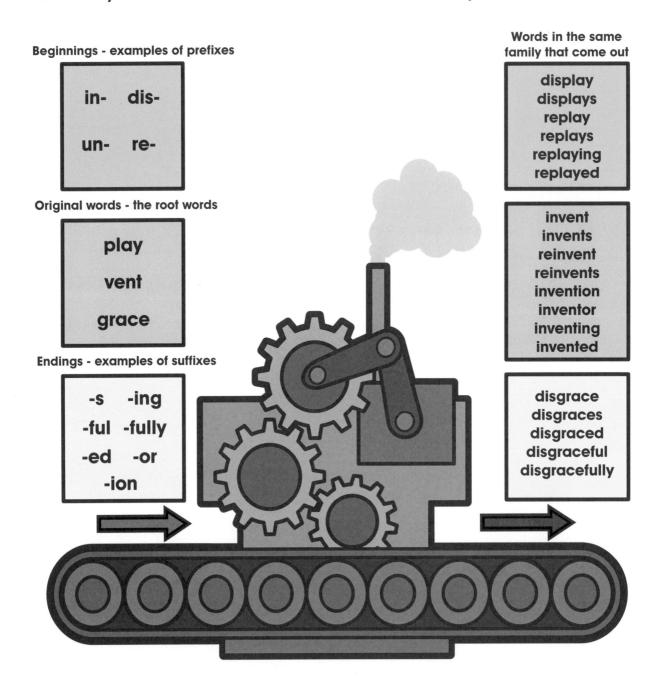

**Beginnings - examples of prefixes**

in-  dis-

un-  re-

**Original words - the root words**

play

vent

grace

**Endings - examples of suffixes**

-s    -ing

-ful  -fully

-ed   -or

-ion

**Words in the same family that come out**

display
displays
replay
replays
replaying
replayed

invent
invents
reinvent
reinvents
invention
inventor
inventing
invented

disgrace
disgraces
disgraced
disgraceful
disgracefully

## Speak about it

What is a prefix? What job does it do?
What is a suffix? What job does it do?
What do all the words in the word family have in common?
Why are they called 'word families'?

## Comprehension

1) When the machine builds new words, does the spelling of the original word change?

2) What is the longest word that the machine has made?

3) How many parts does that word contain?

4) Why is it important to have a dictionary when you are building word families?

5) Can all root words make other words in a family?

## Language focus

1) What is the pattern in these words that makes them a family?

   **attack    back    black    crack    hack    Jack    knack**

2) Build word families out of these words using the prefixes **dis-**, **in-** or **re-**.

   **direct    agree    act**

   Write sentences to show that you understand their meaning. Check your spelling in a dictionary. Does the spelling of the original word change?

3) Build word families out of these words using the suffixes **-ing**, **-d**, **-r** or **-able**.

   **change    read    teach**

   Check your spelling in a dictionary. Does the spelling of the original word change? Write sentences to show that you understand their meaning.

4) How many words can you make in a family using these original words?

   **consider    support    produce    cover    accurate**

   Use prefixes and suffixes. Does the spelling of the original word change? How? Write sentences to show that you understand their meaning.

## Links to writing

1) Imagine that a new person has arrived in your class who does not speak English very well. Write a set of 'handy hints' to help him or her build word families. Make sure he or she knows how to spell the words. Give any rules that will help.

# 3 Myths and legends

***Theseus and the Minotaur*** – a Greek myth

Long ago, on the island of Crete, lived a king called Minos. He hated the people of Athens. They had killed his son. They were at war.

In his palace, trapped in a labyrinth* underground, lived a monster – the Minotaur. This creature was half man and half bull.

King Aegeus of Athens agreed that if Minos would leave Athens alone, Athens would send seven Athenian boys and seven Athenian girls to Crete every nine years to be eaten by the Minotaur as a sacrifice. King Aegeus realised that the only way to stop this was to kill the Minotaur. His brave son Theseus went to see what he could do.

'But the Minotaur is a terrible monster! How can you kill it?' cried his father.

Theseus replied, 'The gods will help me.'

Now, Minos had a beautiful daughter called Ariadne. She fell in love with Theseus and wanted to help him. She knew that if he entered the labyrinth, he would never find his way out and would be killed. She knew the secret of the labyrinth so she went in with a long ball of string and left a sword for him. She let the string trail behind her until it was all used up.

The next day, Theseus went into the labyrinth to do battle with the monster. There was a long and brutal battle, but Theseus killed it with the sword and rescued the children who were to be eaten. He found his way out by following the string that Ariadne had left for him.

Princess Ariadne was waiting for him. They all escaped on Theseus's ship and sailed away.

*labyrinth – something like a maze

## Speak about it

What kind of stories do you expect to find in a myth or a legend?

What kind of people do you expect to find in a myth or a legend?

Think of the legends of Robin Hood or King Arthur. Are legends different from myths?

What other Greek myths do you know?

## Comprehension

1) Where did Minos live?

2) Why did he have a problem with Athens? What had happened in the past?

3) What solution did King Aegeus come up with?

4) Why do you think that Theseus did not like this? What did he plan to do?

5) What was the Minotaur? Where did it live?

6) How did Ariadne help to solve the problem?

## Language focus

1) Read the story again. Copy and complete the chart. This will help you understand what makes a myth special.

| Feature | In this myth | In other myths |
|---|---|---|
| has a hero | | |
| hero overcomes impossible | | |
| good hero wins over evil | | |

2) In other myths and legends, magic is used. Think of another story, for example King Arthur. How is magic used? Is it used for good or evil? How does it change the story?

3) Some myths and legends contain monsters. Do some research. Find out why the Minotaur was in the labyrinth and why he was evil. Write a description of the Minotaur.

## Links to writing

1) Write a play of Theseus and the Minotaur and perform it.

   How might the characters feel?

   How will you set out the playscript? How will it be different from the story here?

   What special effects, scenery and props will you need?

2) Every race has a myth about how it was created.

   Christians have Adam and Eve.

   Native Australians have Dreamtime.

   **Research creation myths, e.g. from the Vikings or from ancient Egypt. Write a version of one of these.**

# 4  Headings and sub-headings

# Skateboarding

### The beginnings of skateboarding

Skateboarding started in the 1930s. Children attached roller skates to a wooden plank. In 1958, the first real skateboard was made in California. Firstly, the shop owner made sets of skate wheels. Then he attached them to square wooden boards. Soon, many young people were rolling down hills and calling it 'sidewalk surfing'.

### Three key points in the history of skateboarding

- The first skateboarding competition was held at a middle school in California in 1964.
- In 1965, the first National Skateboard Championship was on the TV.
- In 1966, the first film was made showing only skateboarders doing tricks. This was called *Skaterdater.*

### Skateboarding today

By the 1970s, over 40 million skateboards were sold in America. Lots of skate parks were opened. A man named Guy Grundy set the speed record on a skateboard of 68 miles per hour. A 2002 report found that there were 18.5 million skateboarders in the world. In 2008, 71 per cent of skaters were 12 to 17 years old. In 2006, 45 per cent were in that age range.

## Speak about it

What is a heading?

What is a sub-heading?

How can you tell the difference between them?

How do they help you understand the passage better?

Why do you think the writer used the bullet points in the middle section?

## Comprehension

1) When did skateboarding start?
2) Where was the first real skateboard made?
3) What did young people first call this sport?
4) List three important things about skateboards that happened in the 1960s.
5) How do you know that skateboarding was an important sport by 1970?
6) Who set the speed record? How fast did he go?

## Language focus

1) A sub-heading tells you what is in the passage under it.
   Make notes about what is in the passage under the **first** sub-heading.
   Ask yourself questions such as: What? When? Who? Why? How?
   Is the sub-heading the right one to use?
2) Do the same with the last paragraph. What other information would you put under this sub-heading?
3) Under the second sub-heading the writer uses bullet points. How do they make it easier to read?
4) Go back to the first section. Write the paragraph using a new bullet for each new point. Is this easier to read?

## Links to writing

1) Choose another passage from a book you are using in class, such as a history topic. Make notes like you did above. You could use a chart.

| Paragraph | Main points |
|-----------|-------------|
| 1 |  |
| 2 |  |

Divide the passage into sections. Use sub-headings.

2) Give this to a partner to read. Would they use different sub-headings? Why?
3) Use a computer to write the passage. Experiment with the size of sub-headings. Should they be in bold? What about colour? How do these things make your work easier to understand?

# 5 Drawing inferences: characters and feelings

**From *The Girl Who Stayed for Half a Week***

Some kids hate their teacher. I nearly hated Miss Baker last year. She always put me down. Look where you're putting your feet, Michael, must your work be so untidy, so messy, Michael, do you have to take up so much room, Michael? I couldn't help being me and sprouting in all directions. I couldn't help growing. I didn't tell myself to grow. I just did. But in the end I didn't hate her … In fact I gave her a box of chocolates at the end of the year, though I didn't choose my favourites and five other kids gave her the same kind.

But Miss is something else. If Miss reads something you've written and she thinks it's good she smiles at the pages before she says anything as if she understands the meaning behind the words you wrote on the page, sad or frightening or funny. She's got grey eyes and curly brown hair and a curly grin with a crooked tooth and she's not very big so I reach things down from the shelves for her, being the tallest in the class, although Greg Grubber is wider.

*Gene Kemp*

## Speak about it

Why do writers include characters in their stories?

Why is it important to tell your reader about how these characters feel?

How can you tell how a character feels?

**Through how he or she acts?**

**What he or she says?**

**How he or she behaves?**

Can you think of examples of these from books that you have read?

## Comprehension

1) What is the name of the main character of this story?

2) Why did he hate his teacher for a time?

3) What was the problem as he was growing up?

4) Why did he change what he thought about Miss Baker?

5) How did he show this at the end of the year?

6) Michael says he didn't choose his favourites. What does this show about him?

## Language focus

1) Using the right words is important if you are trying to show how a character feels. Make two columns with the headings **Feels happy** and **Feels sad**. Put the following words in the correct column. Look up any words that you do not understand.

| | | | | |
|---|---|---|---|---|
| blissful | wretched | elated | desolate | lively |
| anguished | distressed | jovial | mournful | joyous |

2) Use the words in sentences about characters to show that you know what they mean. How would characters act if they felt like this?

3) Write the story from Greg Grubber's point of view. How does he feel about his size? How do people make fun of him? How does he try to get Miss Baker's attention?

## Links to writing

1) Continue the story of Michael and Miss Baker. Show how they become even better friends and why Michael ends up giving her a box of chocolates at the end of the year! Michael could produce an excellent piece of work and Miss Baker might encourage him to put it on the school website.

**What would Greg Grubber say and do?**

**How would Miss Baker persuade Michael?**

**What happens when the writing is published?**

**Why does Michael give Miss Baker his favourite chocolates in the end?**

# 6 Finding your way around reference texts

Let's find out more about reference texts.

Sometimes you have to look up the meaning of hard words. You can look in a *dictionary* or a *thesaurus*.

A **dictionary** is arranged in **alphabetical order**.

> **massage**  1 *n.* act of rubbing or stroking to relieve aches and pains
> 2 *v.* to perform massage
> **massive**  1 *adj.* forming or consisting of a large mass
> 2 *adj.* large of scope or degree
> **mast**  1 *n.* long pole rising from the deck of a ship from which sail can be set
> 2 *n.* vertical pole supporting radio or TV aerial
> 3 *v.* to equip with a mast

It gives the **definitions** (meanings) of words.

It helps us **check the spelling** of **words**.

A **thesaurus** is also arranged in **alphabetical order**.

> **director** instructor, ruler, controller, adviser, manager, master, superintendent, leader, monitor, guide
> **dirt** filth, foulness, sordidness, uncleanness, soil, muck, grime, mud
> **dirty** filthy, foul, sordid, unclean, soiled, mucky, grimy, begrimed, sullied, nasty, squalid

It contains **synonyms** (words with similar meanings).

## Speak about it

Why do people use reference books?

What kinds of reference books do you use at school?

Do you use any reference books at home? What kinds?

How are they different from other books in the way they look on the page?

Where else could you look to find out about meanings of words?

## Comprehension

1) How is a dictionary arranged? How does this help us to find words?

2) What can it help us with?

3) List one other thing dictionaries tell us about words.

4) How is a thesaurus arranged?

5) How is it different from a dictionary in what it tries to do?

6) What is a **synonym**?

## Language focus

1) Imagine that **skin** and **slot** are the first and last words on a dictionary page. Which words from this list would you find on the page? Write them in alphabetical order.

| slum | slang | leigh | skull | slope | skirt | snake | skate |
|------|-------|-------|-------|-------|-------|-------|-------|
| sober | skewer | skid | sloop | slave | slither | social | smile |

2) Find a synonym from the box closest in meaning to each of these.

   **a.** reveal

   **b.** prohibit

   **c.** jovial

   | boats | show | hide | meat | forbid |
   |-------|------|------|------|--------|
   | jolly | allow | sad | quiet | reserved |

3) Find an antonym (a word of opposite meaning) from the box for each of these.

   **a.** absent

   **b.** ancient

   **c.** cautious

   | stupid | present | disappeared | old |
   |--------|---------|-------------|-----|
   | modern | often | reckless | curse | help |

## Links to writing

1) Choose ten words from the activities above that you had to look up in a dictionary or thesaurus. Write them in sentences to show that you understand what they mean.

2) Make up an alphabet quiz to use in class, e.g. *What letter makes honey?* (B). *Which letter allows ships to sail?* (C). *What is the synonym for … ? What is the antonym of … ?*

# 7 Test your grammar, punctuation and spelling

## Grammar

### Determiners

Choose the right determiner in each sentence: *a, an* or *the.*

Use *the*

Use *an* if the next word starts with a vowel (*a e i o u*).

Use *a* if the next word starts with a consonant.

1) The boy in ___ blue coat just ran off with my pen.

2) I'm not sure which one, but ___ girl over there just asked if she could borrow my pencil.

3) ___ orang-utan is orange.

4) ___ chimpanzee wanted a banana.

5) What would you choose to eat. ___ insect or ___ apple?

6) Would you play at home or in ___ best skatepark in town?

### Headings and sub-headings

Plan to write about your pet. Write a title. Write three sub-headings, e.g.:

**Care for your hamster**
*Choosing a cage*
*Food and water*
*Toys to play with*

## Punctuation

**Capital letters, full stops, exclamation marks and question marks**

Rewrite each sentence correctly.

1) zoe and bella could not believe their eyes

2) look out

3) what do you think

4) london, paris and new york are all capital cities

5) january april and december are my favourite months of the year

6) what are you thinking about

## Spelling

### Adding the suffix -ly

Write the new form of the word as an adverb with the suffix **-ly**.

Example   soft → softly

**1)** sad

**2)** different

**3)** usual

**4)** vertical

**5)** angry

**6)** happy

### Exception words

Find a word that rhymes with the first word, and has the same spelling.

Example   past → last

**1)** break

**2)** find

**3)** door

**4)** path

**5)** buy

**6)** rough

# 8  Planning your writing: letters

**Let's investigate letters for a range of different purposes.**

**Letter 1**

The New School,
Bird Lane,
London, N11 11A

30 March 2007

The Manager
Naff Coaches Ltd
Neasden

Dear Sir,

I am writing to complain about poor service from your coach service last week.

My class (3B) were going on a day trip to the Natural History Museum. We only go on three trips a year and everyone was ready to leave at 8.30 a.m.

The coach had been booked by our teacher, Ms Sharpe, three months ago and you were told the time to arrive.

You did not arrive until 10.30 a.m. When you did arrive you did not apologise. You just said that 'there had been a problem'. Many of the boys and girls in my class were disappointed. All you did was to tell them off about making too much noise and eating sweets on the coach.

When we arrived at the museum we were too late for our special talk and so missed the best bits about dinosaurs.

What I want to know is what you are going to do about this? All my class were very upset. We had to pay for the trip but we did not get there in time.

I look forward to your reply.

Yours sincerely,

Mina Patel

Mina Patel

**Letter 2**

School – 31 March 2007

Hi Sophie,

Just had to tell you what happened yesterday – what a mess! You know Ms Sharpe takes us to the museum every year – usually a big yawn – ugh! But it was such a laugh this year.

First the coach didn't turn up. We were waiting hours – and most of us ate our sandwiches. Of course the teachers were going mad. When it did arrive the driver was a real misery guts – all he did was moan, moan, moan ... we all had a laugh on the coach though with Fred's new iPod. Much better listening to the music.

The museum was good, even though we missed the bit with the dinosaurs. Now we're back in school and have to do all that writing! I have to stop Fred copying my work – he never does anything for himself.

Anyway – talk soon. Love n'stuff,

Mina

## Speak about it

Why do people write letters?
Who would be the audience for these letters?
What do you notice about the layout of the letters?

## Comprehension

1) Who is Letter 1 written to? What is its purpose?

2) What happened to make Mina write the letter? Give some examples to prove your point.

3) Which part of the trip were the children really looking forward to?

4) What do you think she expects the coach company to do?

5) Who is Letter 2 written to? What is its purpose?

6) Why is Mina writing this letter? Give some examples to prove your point.

7) What does Letter 2 say about how Mina felt about school trips?

## Language focus

1) Compare the style and layout of the two letters. Use a chart like this one.

|  | Letter 1 | Letter 2 |
|---|---|---|
| Purpose |  |  |
| Tone (how it sounds) | serious, concerned | friendly, jokey |
| Layout |  |  |
| Language used |  |  |

2) Write out these addresses correctly for letters. What rules about setting out addresses can you think of?

   a. 3 lisburne rd belfast nn3 2ds

   b. home farm mill st ambridge borsetshire bs3 2ss

   c. flat 6 docklands buildings admirals sq London w1 2ww

## Links to writing

1) Imagine that you bought a new computer game and it does not work. Write a letter to the company that made it, explaining that you want to replace it. You could use the computer to write and print it.

2) Write a letter to a penfriend who lives overseas, explaining all about your new game and what happened when you realised that it did not work.

# 9 Planning your writing: instructions

**What do you need to know in order to write good instructions? Let's investigate!**

## The line trick

Follow these instructions and you will be able to convince your friends that they cannot believe their eyes!

You'll need a pencil, a piece of paper and a ruler.

**1** Draw two lines the same length. Label the lines **A** and **B**.

Line **A**    Line **B**

**2** Draw lines at the top and bottom of the first line (Line A), like this:

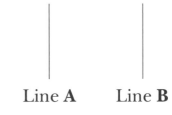

**3** Draw lines at the top and bottom of the other line (Line B), like this:

**4** Show people the lines, side by side.

Say, 'Is Line **A** or Line **B** the longer, or are the two lines the same length?'

Most people think Line **B** is longer. They are wrong! The lines at the top and bottom just make it look longer. Let them measure the lines to show that they are the same length.

### Speak about it

Why might we need to use instructions?

What would we be trying to do?

How is the layout of instructions often different from other kinds of text?

Do these features help in making instructions better? How?

## Comprehension

1) What is the aim of these instructions?
2) How long should you draw the first two lines?
3) What are you told to add to these two lines after this?
4) What do people think when they see the lines?
5) How do they test that they are wrong?
6) How many instructions are you given? How do you know this?

## Language focus

1) Investigate the features of instructions. Copy and complete a chart like this.

| Feature | Example |
|---|---|
| What is the aim? | |
| What do you need? | |
| What are the steps? | |
| How do you know? | |
| What kinds of verbs are used? | Commands: **Draw** lines ... **show** people ... |
| Who is being given the instructions? | |

## Links to writing

1) Write a set of instructions explaining how to make something, such as a paper aeroplane.
   **Why are you making it? What do you need to make it?**
   **How will you make it – step by step?**
   **How will you test whether it works?**
   **Which other features will you use?**

2) Write other kinds of instructions, e.g. how to find your way from school to home, to give to a new friend who is visiting.
   **Do you use different features?**
   **How important is it to get the facts correct and in the right order?**
   **Will a diagram be helpful?**

# 10 Planning your writing: leaflets

5,000 square feet of jungle paradise

The largest tropical house in the area

Walk amongst beautifully coloured butterflies and lots of other animals too.

We are situated on Sykes Lane Car park, on the A606 Oakham to Stamford Road, near the village of Empingham. Tourist signposted from the road.

## Why not visit us soon?

The Butterfly Farm
Sykes Lane Car Park, Empingham
North Shore Rutland Water
Oakham, Rutland LE15 8PX
Tel & Fax: 01780 460515
www.rutlandwaterbutterflyfarm.co.uk
Schools and other groups are our speciality. Please call for details.
Open every day from 1st April until 31st October from 10.30-17.00
last admissions half an hour before closing
10.30-16.30 in September and October

## Rutland Water Butterfly Farm

From the heart of England, to the heart of the jungle.....a totally tropical treat

## An amazing world of contrasts awaits you

From babbling brook to the mighty reservoir, all the fish of the area are housed in the impressive Aquatic Centre.

Here can you see at close quarters the huge Carp of the lake as well as all the other coarse and game fish of the area in one of the finest freshwater Aquariums.

In the Aquatic Centre, the hidden world of Rutland Water is no longer hidden.

inside the 5,000 square feet of tropical jungle

part of the aquatic display

## Inside the Tropical House

Walk through the doors and be transported into five thousand square feet of tropical paradise. Hundreds of brilliantly coloured butterflies fly around you whilst the parrots and other birds look on.

In the ponds, large Koi carp swim around whilst the terrapins sun themselves on the sides.

Look for the Iguana lizards up in the trees and many other animals such as stick insects and Giant African land Snails in the undergrowth.

The tropical house is designed with everybody in mind, prams and wheelchairs will have no problems on our completely flat slabbed pathways.

## A great visit - everytime

Young and old alike will be enthralled by this magical environment. Will you be lucky enough to see the marvel of a butterfly emerging from its pupa? Maybe one will even land on your head. One thing is for sure, no two visits are the same. Maybe this is why visitors return time and again.

### The Twilight Zone

Our newest attraction. Safely housed behind glass are some of the world's mini-beasts. From huge tarantula spiders to poisonous scorpions.... dare you enter? Will you leave wanting to cuddle a cockroach?

### Other facilities

We have a large car park and just yards from the centre you will find a cafe, children's adventure playground and toilets. Don't forget Europe's largest man made lake, with all that has to offer.

## Speak about it

What is a leaflet?

Why do people write them?

Where do you get leaflets from?

What do you notice is different about the layout of a leaflet from other kinds of text?

## Comprehension

1) Who is this leaflet aimed at? What does it aim to do?

2) What does the writer mean by a 'world of contrasts'?

3) Where are all the fish living at this farm?

4) Use a dictionary to find the meaning of these hard words.

   **a.** babbling   **b.** reservoir   **c.** impressive   **d.** aquatic   **e.** paradise

5) How large is the 'jungle paradise'?

## Language focus

1) Investigate the features of leaflets. Draw and complete a chart.

| Feature | Example |
| --- | --- |
| Audience | |
| Big, bold text | |
| Short paragraphs | |
| Use of pictures | |
| Main headings or headlines | |
| Talks to you | |

2) Why do you think pictures are used in this leaflet? What information do they add? How do they make the leaflet appealing to the audience?

3) Write the words and phrases that would persuade you to go to the butterfly farm. Say why.

## Links to writing

1) Design and write a leaflet about a local place you know – a park, theme park or a sea-life centre.
   **Who is your audience? What are you trying to do?**
   **Where will you find the right information? Who will you ask?**
   **What features will be important in the design?**
   **You could use the computer to design and print the leaflet – and even try it out on any new pupils.**

# 11 Suffixes with vowels

**You can make spelling mistakes when you add a suffix.**
**Let's find some rules to help.**

*In* The Pied Piper of Hamelin, *Robert Browning tells the story of how a Piper leads away all the children in the town. He plays music and the children follow. Here are some lines from the poem.*

## Adapted from *The Pied Piper of Hamelin*

Small feet were patter**ing**, wooden shoes clatter**ing**,
Little hands clapp**ing**, and little tongues chatter**ing**,

Out came all the children runn**ing**.
All the little boys and girls,
With rosy cheeks and golden curls,
And sparkl**ing** eyes and teeth like pearls,

Tripp**ing** and skipp**ing**, ran merrily after
The wonderful music with shouting and laughter.

### Speak about it

What is a **suffix**?
Where do you find them in words?
Which suffix is in **bold** in the poem?
Which type of words is it being added to?
Does the spelling of the original words change when you add a suffix?
Which words do you not know the meaning of? Find their meanings in a dictionary.

## Comprehension

1) What were the small feet doing?

2) What kind of shoes are these children wearing?

3) The poet says that the children are like 'fowl in the farmyard' as they run into the street. Write down the name of two kinds of animals that we call **fowl**.

4) List at least two verbs that the poet uses to show how the children moved.

5) Look in the passage and find words ending in **-ing**. Which root words have more than one syllable? Can you see any pattern?

## Language focus

1) Add the suffix **-ly** to these words. What happens to the spelling? Check your answers in a dictionary. Can you make a rule?

   **complete**    **usual**    **final**    **cruel**    **careless**

2) Add the suffix **-ly** to these words. What happens to the spelling? Check your answers in a dictionary. Can you make a rule?

   **gentle**    **simple**    **humble**    **noble**

3) Add the suffix **-ly** to these words. What happens to the spelling? Check your answers in a dictionary. Can you make a rule?

   **basic**    **frantic**    **dramatic**    **angry**    **happy**

   Are there any exceptions? Try it with 'public'.

## Links to writing

1) Write the first lines of the poem. Change **-ing** words to **-ed** words, e.g.: **pattering** → **pattered**. What else has to change in the sentences to make them correct?

2) Think about what you have learned about adding suffixes starting with a vowel. Write some rules for a poster. Find new words to give examples.

# 12 Prefixes

What happens to the spelling of words when you add prefixes?
Let's investigate!

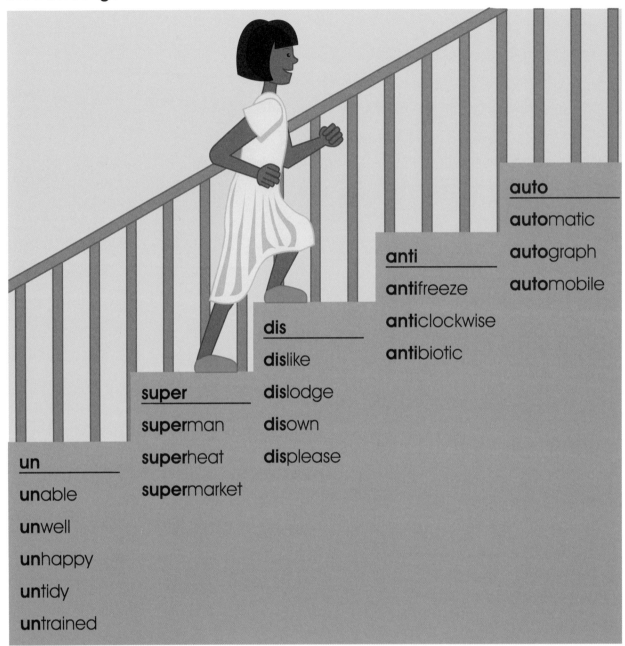

**auto**

**auto**matic

**auto**graph

**auto**mobile

**anti**

**anti**freeze

**anti**clockwise

**anti**biotic

**dis**

**dis**like

**dis**lodge

**dis**own

**dis**please

**super**

**super**man

**super**heat

**super**market

**un**

**un**able

**un**well

**un**happy

**un**tidy

**un**trained

### Speak about it

What is a prefix?

What does the prefix pre- mean?

How does knowing this tell you what a prefix does?

Does adding prefixes change the meaning of a word? Explain how.

Are there any words that you do not understand? Use a dictionary to find their meanings.

## Comprehension

1) Prefixes mean something. You can tell this by looking at what the words on the opposite page have in common. What do you think **anti-** means?

2) How does adding **un-** to a word change its meaning?

3) Try saying the words opposite without the prefix. Which word is no longer complete?

4) Which words in the list opposite mean these phrases?

**put in your car engine to stop it freezing**

**a place where you can buy lots of different foods and drinks**

**works by itself**

## Language focus

1) Add the prefix **dis-** to the following words. Write the words and check the spelling. Does the original word change its spelling?

   **a.** qualify      **b.** agree      **c.** appear      **d.** connect

2) Look in a dictionary to find the meaning of these words: supernatural, supercharge. What does the prefix **super-** mean? When you add it to a root word, does it change the spelling?

3) Look in a dictionary to find the meaning of these words: autobiography, automate. What does the prefix **auto-** mean? When you add it to a root word, does it change the spelling?

4) Add the prefix **anti-** to these words: septic, social. Does the original word change its spelling? Use the words in sentences to show their meaning.

5) The prefix **sub-** means 'under'; **inter-** means 'between' or 'among'. Use a dictionary. Find three new words containing each of these prefixes. Write the words and check the spelling.

## Links to writing

1) Which of the following words have the wrong prefix? Use a dictionary. Write the words correctly.

   **a.** disofficial      **b.** uninfect      **c.** dishonest      **d.** deflate

   **e.** dissocial      **f.** autoheat      **g.** antihappy

2) Write some rules about prefixes to help when writing.

**What are they? How can they help with word meanings?**

# 13 Poems to perform

### Ten white snowmen

Ten white snowmen standing in a line,
One toppled over, then there were nine.

Nine white snowmen standing up straight.
One lost his balance, then there were eight.

Eight white snowmen in a snowy heaven,
The wind blew one over, then there were seven.

Seven white snowmen with pipes made of sticks,
One slumped to the ground, then there were six.

Six white snowmen standing on the drive,
One got knocked down, then there were five.

Five white snowmen outside the front door,
An icicle fell on one, then there were four.

Four white snowmen standing by the tree,
One slipped and fell apart, then there were
three.

Three white snowmen underneath the yew,
One crumbled overnight, then there were two.

Two white snowmen standing in the sun,
One melted right down, then there was one.

One white snowman standing all alone,
Vanished without trace, then there were none.

*John Foster*

**Speak about it**

How does each verse start?
What happens in the story at the end of each verse?
How does each verse rhyme?
What do you notice about the pattern of this poem?

## Comprehension

1) How many snowmen does the poem start with? How many are there at the end?
2) What happened to make eight snowmen?
3) What happened to make five snowmen?
4) What happened to make one snowman?
5) What do you think happened to the last one?
6) What happens to the word 'snowmen' when there is only one left?

## Language focus

1) Read the first line of the poem in four ways. Stress the word in bold. How does it change the meaning? Which is the best way?

   **Ten** white snowmen standing in a line,

   Ten **white** snowmen standing in a line,

   Ten white **snowmen** standing in a line,

   Ten white snowmen **standing** in a line,

2) Read the second line of the poem. Be quiet when the words are underlined. Be loud when the words are in **bold**. Which is the best way?

   One toppled over, **then there were nine**.

   **One toppled over**, then there were nine.

3) Read the first verse. Use what you have learned about the best way to say the lines. Try this for the second verse as well.
4) Hold up your hands to show your fingers. As you say each verse, hide one finger. How does this help your presentation?

## Links to writing

1) Write a poem using the same pattern. Start at ten, e.g.:

| Number | Adjective | Noun |
|---|---|---|
| ten | jumping | frogs |

End each verse with '... **and then there were** ...'

You will have to find words to rhyme with the numbers. Use a chart to collect them.

| Numbers | Rhyming words |
|---|---|
| ten | hen, men, den ... |
| nine | fine, wine, mine ... |

2) Present your poem. Ask others how well the poem has been performed.

# 14 Test your grammar, punctuation and spelling

### Using conjunctions to express time and cause

Choose a conjunction to fill the gap. These words may help you: *when, before, after, while, because.*

**1)** I always say thank you _____ someone opens a door for me.

**2)** I eat _____ I am hungry.

**3)** I brush my teeth _____ I go to bed.

**4)** I smile _____ I am happy.

**5)** I like to whistle _____ I work.

**6)** I feel better _____ I have eaten my breakfast.

### Using adverbs to express time and cause

Choose an adverb to fill the gap. These words may help you: *firstly, then, next, soon, so.*

**How to make jelly**

**1)** _____, choose a jelly flavour you like.

**2)** Break it into pieces and _____ pour boiling water onto it.

**3)** _____ stir it ___ that that there are no lumps left.

**4)** Leave it for about 15 minutes ___ that it cools.

**5)** _____ put it in the fridge to set.

**6)** _____ you will be able to enjoy your jelly.

### Using commas in lists

Write a list of your four favourite …

meals:

animals:

sports:

E.g.: **meals: pizza, lasagne, fish pie and chicken stew**

## Spelling

### Word endings that sound like /zhun/

Choose and write out the correct spelling for each one.

**Example**

| division | divishion | devision |
|---|---|---|

| | | | |
|---|---|---|---|
| **1)** | confuzion | confusion | confuson |
| **2)** | decision | desicion | decisen |
| **3)** | telivision | teleevizun | television |
| **4)** | collicion | collision | colision |
| **5)** | invasion | invazun | envasion |
| **6)** | occasion | ockasion | ocassion |

### Suffix -ous

Write each word with the suffix **-ous.**

Add -ous no change
Add -ous but drop the last *e* first
Add -ous but change *y* to *i*

**Example** danger → dangerous

**1)** nerve
**2)** fame
**3)** vary
**4)** fury
**5)** courage

# 15  Planning your writing: correct order, sequence

**From *Mr Croc Gets Fit***

*Frank Rogers*

**Speak about it**

What is the correct order for a story? Is there one?

Why is the correct order important in stories?

What would happen if stories were not always in the correct order?

How do you know that this story is in the correct order?

Is there a way of telling this story in a different order?

# RISING STARS

## English Study Guide: Year 3

## Answer Booklet

### 1 Tricky spelling

**Comprehension**

1) take, appear, necessary, miss, grace, appoint
2) mis-, dis-, un-
3) dis-, un-
4) -ing, -ful
5) mistake, disappearing, unnecessary, missing, disgraceful, disappoint
6) no

**Language focus**

1) mistake, disapprove, indefinite, reopen, refresh, dissatisfied, intake, retake
   The spelling of the root word does not change.
2) The spelling of the root word does not change (apart from excite > exciting).
3) completing, behaving, replacing, approving, hoping
   Drop the final -e before adding -ing. This is because /ei/ makes a different sound.

**Links to writing**

1), 2) *Own answers*

### 2 Building from root words

**Comprehension**

1) No, not the words in this machine.
2) dis – grace – ful – ly
3) four
4) To find more words and to check spelling. Some phonemes may sound the same as others but be spelled differently.
5) No – this is why you have to be careful.

**Language focus**

1) They all contain the -ack family.
2) indirect, redirect; disagree; react
   The spelling should not change. Just add the prefix.
   Accept all correct and reasonable sentences.
3) changing, changer, changed, changeable; reading, readable; teaching, teachable. NOTE: change. Drop the final -e when adding -ing. Accept all correct and reasonable sentences.
4) Many answers possible, including: considering, considered, reconsider, considerable; supporting; production, producing, produced, reproduce; discover, covering, coverable; inaccurate, accurately. Note spelling rules above. Accept all correct and reasonable sentences.

**Links to writing**

1), 2) *Own answers*

### 3 Myths and legends

**Comprehension**

1) Crete
2) His son had been killed by the people of Athens.
3) Seven boys and seven girls would be sent for sacrifice by the Minotaur every nine years.
4) This was cruel. Theseus planned to kill the monster.
5) It was half man, half bull. It lived in the labyrinth.
6) She enabled Theseus to find his way out of the labyrinth (with string) and to kill the Minotaur (with a sword) and escape.

**Language focus**

1)

| Feature | In this myth | In other myths |
|---|---|---|
| has a hero | yes | *Own answers* |
| hero overcomes impossible | yes | *Own answers* |
| good hero wins over evil | yes | *Own answers* |

2) *Own answer.* The legend of King Arthur contains magic with Merlin and the Lady of the Lake, and shows good overcoming evil via the Knights of the Round Table.
3) *Own answer*

**Links to writing**

1), 2) *Own answers*

### 4 Headings and sub-headings

**Comprehension**

1) In the 1930s.
2) California
3) 'Sidewalk surfing'
4) The first skateboarding competition was in 1964.
   The first National Skateboard Championship was in 1965.
   The first film showing only skateboarding tricks was in 1966.
5) Over 40 million skateboards were sold in America.
6) Guy Grundy set the speed record by travelling 68 mph.

**Language focus**

1) The first sub-heading gives information about where, when and how skateboarding started many years ago.
2) The final paragraph gives facts and figures about skateboarding today. *Own answers*
3) Bullet points split up the text and the bullet draws your eye to each separate point. This makes it easier to understand.
4) *Own answer*

**Links to writing**

1), 2), 3) *Own answers*

### 5 Drawing inferences: characters and feelings

**Comprehension**

1) Michael
2) She always put him down.
3) He took up a lot of room.
4) She appreciated the stories he wrote.
5) He gave her a box of chocolates.
6) *Own answer*

**Language focus**

1)

| Feels happy | Feels sad |
|---|---|
| blissful | wretched |
| elated | desolate |
| lively | anguished |
| jovial | distressed |
| joyous | mournful |

2), 3) *Own answers*

### 6 Finding your way around reference texts

**Comprehension**

1) Alphabetically, so that words are in a predictable order.
2) Meaning and spelling.
3) What type of word it is.
4) Alphabetically
5) It gives synonyms, but not the actual meaning.
6) A word with a similar meaning.

**Language focus**

1) skirt, skull, slang, slave, slither, sloop, slope
2) a. show
   b. forbid
   c. jolly
3) a. present
   b. modern
   c. reckless

**Links to writing**

1) *Own answers*

### 7 Test your grammar, punctuation and spelling

**Grammar**

*Determiners*

1) The boy in **the** blue coat just ran off with my pen.
2) I'm not sure which one, but **a** girl over there just asked if she could borrow my pencil.
3) **An** orang-utan is orange.
4) **The** chimpanzee wanted a banana.
5) What would you choose to eat: **an** insect or **an** apple?
6) Would you play at home or in **the** best skatepark in town?

*Headings and sub-headings*

Accept all correct and reasonable attempts.

## Punctuation

### Capital letters, full stops, exclamation marks and question marks

1) Zoe and Bella could not believe their eyes.
2) Look out!
3) What do you think?
4) London, Paris and New York are all capital cities.
5) January, April and December are my favourite months of the year.
6) What are you thinking about?

## Spelling

### Adding the suffix -ly

1) sadly
2) differently
3) usually
4) vertically
5) angrily
6) happily

### Exception words

1) break > steak
2) find > mind
3) door > poor
4) path > bath
5) buy > guy
6) rough > tough

## 8  Planning your writing: letters

### Comprehension

1) Letter 1 is written to Naff Coaches Ltd, to complain about poor service.
2) Mina Patel wrote the letter because the coach arrived two hours late: 'everyone was ready to leave at 8.30 a.m.', 'You did not arrive until 10.30 a.m.'.
3) A special talk about dinosaurs.
4) Refund some of the money paid for the c oach.
5) Letter 2 is written to Mina's friend Sophie to describe her day and to entertain.
6) Mina is writing this letter to share what happened to her: 'Just had to tell you what happened'.
7) Mina enjoyed the trip: 'it was such a laugh this year', 'we all had a laugh on the coach', 'The museum was good'.

### Language focus

1)

| | Letter 1 | Letter 2 |
|---|---|---|
| Purpose | persuade, inform | describe, entertain |
| Tone | serious, concerned | friendly, jokey |
| Layout | full address paragraphs | partial address paragraphs |
| Language used | formal | informal |

2) 3 Lisburne Road,
Belfast,
NN3 2DS

Home Farm,
Mill Street,
Ambridge,
Borsetshire,
BS3 2SS

Flat 6,
Docklands Buildings,
Admirals Square,
London,
W1 2WW

Always use capital letters for place names and postcodes.
Put each section of the address on a different line.

### Links to writing

1), 2) Own answers

## 9  Planning your writing – instructions

### Comprehension

1) The aim of the instructions is teaching how to perform the line trick.
2) The same length.
3) Lines at the top and bottom of the lines.
4) 'Most people think Line B is longer.'
5) By measuring the lines themselves.
6) Four steps, because they are numbered.

### Language focus

1)

| Feature | Example |
|---|---|
| What is the aim? | To perform the line trick. |
| What do you need? | Pencil, a piece of paper and a ruler. |
| What are the steps? | Draw two lines the same length. |
| How do you know? | There are illustrations. |
| What kind of verbs are used? | Commands: **Draw** lines … **show** people … |
| Who is being given the instructions? | Anyone reading them and wanting to learn the trick. |

### Links to writing

1), 2) Own answers

## 10 Planning your writing: leaflets

### Comprehension

1) The leaflet is aimed at possible visitors to inform them about the farm and persuade them to come.
2) Different types of environments close together.
3) The Aquatic Centre.
4) a. To make continuous, murmuring sounds.
   b. A place where water is collected and stored for use.
   c. Having the ability to impress the mind.
   d. Of, in, or pertaining to water.
   e. A place of extreme beauty, delight, or happiness.
5) 5000 square feet

### Language focus

1)

| Feature | Example |
|---|---|
| Audience | Why not visit us soon? |
| Big, bold text | A great visit – everytime |
| Short paragraphs | In the ponds, large Koi carp swim around whilst the terrapins sun themselves on the sides. |
| Use of pictures | Lots of pictures of butterflies |
| Main headings or headlines | The Twilight Zone |
| Talks to you | An amazing world of contrasts awaits you |

2) Pictures are used to give the reader an idea of what the farm is like, allowing them to imagine themselves there and making it more likely for them to visit.
3) Own answer

### Links to writing

1) Own answer

## 11 Suffixes with vowels

### Comprehension

1) pattering
2) wooden shoes
3) chickens, ducks
4) running, skipping, tripping
5) Single-syllable words with a vowel before the final consonant double the final consonant when adding a suffix. Run – running.

### Language focus

1) completely, usually, finally, cruelly, carelessly. Just add the suffix and the spelling does not change unless the word ends in an -l and then this doubles.
2) gently, simply, humbly, nobly. Drop the final -e. The final syllable is stressed in these words.
3) basically, frantically, dramatically, angrily, happily. If it ends in -y, drop the final letter and add the suffix. If it ends in -c, add -ally. Publicly – just add the suffix.

### Links to writing

1) The tense has the change, e.g.: small feet pattered, wooden shoes clattered, little hands clapped, and little tongues chattered.
2), 3) Own answers

## 12 Prefixes

### Comprehension

1) Re- means 'again'.
2) Un- means 'not'.
3) In the auto group, -matic is not a complete word.
4) put in your car engine to stop it freezing – antifreeze
   a place where you can buy lots of different foods and drinks – supermarket
   works by itself – automatic

### Language focus

1) The original spelling does not change.
   a. disqualify    c. disappear
   b. disagree      d. disconnect
2) supernatural: greater than nature, beyond our understanding of the laws of nature; supercharge: a larger charge than usual. Super- means 'more than' or 'beyond'.
   It does not change the spelling of the root word.
3) autobiography: life story written by yourself; automate: to make something work by itself. Auto- means 'self' or 'by one's self'.
   It does not change the spelling of the root word.
4) antiseptic; antisocial. The spelling does not change. Own answers
5) E.g.: submarine, subway; international, interfaith.

### Links to writing

1) a. unofficial       e. antisocial
   b. disinfect        f. superheat
   c. dishonest        g. unhappy
   d. deflate
2) Own answer

**5)** *Own answer*
**6)** dizzy
**Language focus**
**1), 2), 3)** *Own answers*
**Links to writing**
**1), 2)** *Own answers*

## 27 Choosing the best vocabulary and grammar – verbs and adverbs

**Comprehension**
1) '*He lived over the hill behind the town*'.
2) He blew the smoke down into the mill and it was unpopular because the men '*coughed*' and '*spluttered*'.
3) He rang the schoolhouse bell half an hour early. The children would not have liked this because they would have had to rush their breakfasts and arrive early for school.
4) The waves the Giant caused swamped his boats or smashed them on the bank.
5) The giant could lean over into a chimney, he could reach the schoolhouse bell and he made great waves in the river. *Own answer*

**Language focus**
1) a. Deep **beneath** the earth lived a huge dragon.
   b. I found the secret map **under** a large pile of paper.
   c. The beetle scuttled **across** the table in front of me.
   d. I ran **after** the ball, but it rolled in the river.
2), 3) *Own answers*
4) Leaned <u>over</u>, blew <u>down</u>, hanging <u>high</u>; *own answers*

**Links to writing**
1) *Own answers*

## 28 Test your grammar, punctuation and spelling

**Grammar**

*The perfect form of verbs*

| The past tense: *Last week...* | The present perfect: *...this morning* |
|---|---|
| I ran | I have run |
| He kicked | He has kicked |
| She threw | She has thrown |
| We cheered | We have cheered |
| They scored | They have scored |

*What is it?*
1) consonants
2) adverb
3) vowels
4) adverb
5) preposition
6) prefix
7) connective
8) connective
9) prefix

**Punctuation**

*Inverted commas (speech marks)*
1) I looked up and shouted, 'Get me out of here!'
2) She smiled at me and said, 'Will you be my friend?'
3) The dog barked at me when I said, 'Here, boy!'
4) 'You can never tell with animals,' she yelled, 'but trust me, this one is safe.'
5) 'Are you coming with me or not?' she asked.
6) 'If you are in yellow group,' she shouted, 'stand with me.'

**Spelling**

*Adding prefixes*
interact, disappear, superhero, misbehave, autograph, impossible, irregular, illegible

*Useful words*
1) The situation is very peculiar.
2) You describe what we did yesterday in the playground.
3) When swimming you have to learn to breathe well.
4) I thought it was a good idea.
5) Famous people often have a bodyguard.
6) The teacher said we had a surprise.

## Language focus

**1)**

| Paragraph | Detail in it |
|---|---|
| 1 | The main characters. They have an argument. |
| 2 | The Sun demonstrates his power. |
| 3 | The Wind demonstrates his power. |
| 4 | A farmer suggests a final challenge. |
| 5 | They agree to the challenge. |
| 6 | The Wind fails. |
| 7 | The Sun is victorious. |
| 8 | The moral of the story. |

**2)** Yes, a new paragraph should begin when the time, setting or scene changes, or when a new character starts speaking.

**3)** A crow was dying of thirst. He saw a big jug of water on the ground.
When he came up to it, there was only a little water in the bottom. He tried to overturn the jug, but it was too heavy.
At last he saw some small stones. He threw them into the jug until the water level rose. He then drank to his heart's content.
This proves that if you are clever you will be successful in the end.

### Links to writing
**1)** *Own answer*

## 21 Test your grammar, punctuation and spelling

### Grammar

*Using prepositions to express time and cause*

**1)** **During** my lunch break, I chat with my friends.
**2)** We are not allowed to eat our snack **before** playtime.
**3)** We feel rested **after** the summer holidays.
**4)** We have to stay behind at lunchtime **because** we were chatting too much.
**5)** **In** tricky lessons we can work with a friend.
**6)** It's home time **in** ten minutes; hooray!

### *Word families*

| Base word | Word 1 – adjective | Word 2 – noun | Word 3 – adverb |
|---|---|---|---|
| music | musical | musician | musically |
| science | scientific | scientist | scientifically |
| mathematics | mathematical | mathematician | mathematically |
| history | historical | historian | historically |
| art | artistic | artist | artistically |
| geography | geographical | geographer | geographically |

### Punctuation

*Contractions*

**1)** I am
**2)** does not
**3)** will not
**4)** did not
**5)** might have
**6)** should have
**7)** it is/has
**8)** cannot

## Spelling

### *Words ending in /zhuh/ or /chuh/*

**1)** treasure
**2)** furniture
**3)** creature
**4)** picture
**5)** mixture

### *Root words ending in -tch or -ch plus -er*

**1)** teacher
**2)** stretcher
**3)** richer
**4)** catcher
**5)** butcher
**6)** watcher

## 22 Paragraphs 2

### Comprehension

**1)** He visited because he is studying Invaders and Settlers in history.
**2)** Romans, Anglo-Saxons and Vikings.
**3)** They came in the 8th century to around 1100.
**4)** Boudicca fought the Romans and was killed.
**5)** Vikings didn't wear helmets with horns and Roman soldiers didn't like Britain because it was too cold.
**6)** Yes, each paragraph is about a single topic with a topic sentence telling us what the paragraph will be about, followed by sentences telling us more about the topic sentence.

### Language focus

**1)** The topic sentence introduces the paragraph and tells the reader what the paragraph will be about.
**2)** 'To make toast with a toaster is very easy' is the topic sentence because it introduces the paragraph and lets you know what the paragraph will be about.
To make toast with a toaster is very easy.
Before you can switch it on, you need to push down the handle so the bread goes into the toaster.
Switch it on.
You'll need to turn the dial on the toaster to the right time.
Place some bread in the slots in the toaster.
When the toast is ready, it will pop up.

### Links to writing
**1)**, **2)** *Own answers*

## 23 Punctuation of direct speech

### Comprehension

**1)** He says Alice's name is stupid.
**2)** On a wall.
**3)** He would be safer in the ground because she knows he will fall off the wall.
**4)** He thinks she has been listening secretly.
**5)** She has read the traditional nursery rhyme in a book.

### Language focus

**1)** Answers can include:
"<u>Must a name mean something?</u>" Alice asked doubtfully.
"<u>I know,</u>" said Alice.
"<u>Now I declare, that's too bad!</u>" Humpty Dumpty cried.
"<u>I haven't indeed.</u>" Alice replied very gently.

**2) a.** Fred said, "I feel happy today."
**b.** "My team didn't win again," sighed Ranjit.
**c.** "Have you ever been to Australia?" asked Tracy.
**3) a.** "I want a drink," said Tracy.
**b.** "How many sweets have you taken?" asked Fred.
**c.** "That's not fair if you've got more money!" said Harry.

### Links to writing
**1)**, **2)** *Own answer*

## 24 Using connectives

### Comprehension

**1)** *Own answer*
**2)** Cycling makes you healthier.
**3)** More time using a bicycle.
**4)** Sitting in front of computers.
**5)** Useful bike information.
**6)** *'It's often hard to find what you want' about biking.*

### Language focus

**1)** Without connectives, the passage would be very jerky and difficult to read. Connectives help the writing flow.
**2) a.** when/because
**b.** although **c.** while

### Links to writing
**1)** *Own answer*

## 25 Clauses

### Comprehension

**1)** The first postage stamp appeared on May 1, 1840.
**2)** Rowland Hill was once a schoolmaster.
**3)** Before Rowland Hill's stamps, the person who received the letter was the person who paid for the postage.
**4)** Postal rates could be very high, so poor people would 'dread' receiving a letter because they would have to pay for it.
**5)** The new system required the sender to pay in advance by attaching a stamp to their mail; it was also much cheaper.
**6)** The first stamps did not have perforations.
**7)** 'Private postal service' are the words that tell us that the service was not run by the government.

### Language focus

**1)** *'So as to make the sender of a letter responsible for the postage, Hill suggested that it should be paid in advance, by sticking the stamp on the letter.'* Clauses are at the start and end of this sentence.
*'… a private postal service, working in New York, issued a stamp …'* The clause is in the middle here.
**2)**, **3)** *Own answers*

### Links to writing
**1)** *Own answer*

## 26 Choosing the best vocabulary and grammar – adjectives

### Comprehension

**1)** So she could get outside quickly to play in the snow.
**2)** Because the scarf was itchy.
**3)** 'thick' and 'soft'
**4)** She 'poked her finger into the clean snow'.

## 13 Poems to perform

### Comprehension

1) Ten at the beginning. None at the end.
2) One lost his balance.
3) One got knocked down.
4) One melted.
5) It vanished without trace – presumably melted away.
6) The singular of 'snowmen' is 'snowman'.

### Language focus

1), 2), 3), 4) *Own answers*

### Language focus

1), 2), 3), 4) *Own answers*

### Links to writing

1), 2) *Own answers*

## 14 Test your grammar, punctuation and spelling

### Grammar

*Using conjunctions to express time and cause*

1) I always say thank you **when** someone opens a door for me.
2) I eat **when/because** I am hungry.
3) I brush my teeth **before/when** I go to bed.
4) I smile **because/when** I am happy.
5) I like to whistle **while/when** I work.
6) I feel better **after/when** I have eaten my breakfast.

*Using adverbs to express time and cause*

1) **Firstly**, choose a jelly flavour you like.
2) Break it into pieces and **then** pour boiling water onto it.
3) **Next** stir it **so** that that there are no lumps left.
4) Leave it for about 15 minutes **so that** it cools.
5) **Then** put it in the fridge to set.
6) **Soon** you will be able to enjoy your jelly.

### Punctuation

*Using commas in lists*

Ensure pupils have used commas and *and* as shown in the example.

### Spelling

*Words ending in /zhun/*

1) confusion
2) decision
3) television
4) collision
5) invasion
6) occasion

*Suffix -ous*

1) nervous
2) famous
3) various
4) furious
5) courageous

## 15 Planning your writing: correct order, sequence

### Comprehension

1) From television
2) Stretch up./Run on the spot./Touch your toes.
3) Touching his toes makes him burp.
4) There is a text box saying 'NEXT MORNING'.
5) Because he's still wearing his pyjamas.
6) Even though he remembers the other things, he forgets to change out of his pyjamas.

### Language focus

1), 2), 3) *Own answers*
4) *'first'*, *'then'*, *'while'*, *'before'* and *'after'* are all connectives that suggest time passing and then a sequence.

### Links to writing

1), 2) *Own answers*

## 16 Planning your writing: problem solving

### Comprehension

1) A soup factory. He was called Ashley.
2) He fell into a vat of tomato soup.
3) A daring diver.
4) It was infected by radioactive cosmic dust.
5) To draw the reader's attention and make the story more interesting.
6) It tells you the story continues.

### Language focus

1) *Own answer*
2)

| Beginning | Introduces the main character. |
| Middle | Tells us how he became soup boy. |
| End | We don't know! |

3), 4) *Own answers*

### Links to writing

1), 2) *Own answers*

## 17 Capturing imagination – words and phrases

### Comprehension

1) The door 'sprang open'.
2) A spider 'went silently creeping …'.
3) *'huge'*, *'squeezed'*
4) 'shiny horned cows'
5) The frogs were 'as big as men' with 'enormous feet'.
6) They moved in a 'slow, silent procession'.

### Language focus

1) It is more difficult to make a picture in your mind.
2) *Own answer*
3) The adverbs *'silently'* and *'barely'* give extra description to the verb.
4) *Own answer*

### Links to writing

1), 2) *Own answers*

## 18 Predicting what might happen

### Comprehension

1) Little Red Riding Hood
2) Little Red Riding Hood, the Big Bad Wolf and Grandmother. Yes, because they act the same as in the traditional story.
3) *Own answer*
4) Singing or talking rhythmically with rhyming words.
5) Yes, some of the words rhyme: 'wood' and 'hood', 'away' and 'day', 'plan' and 'ran', 'bed' and 'red'.
6) The events happen much more quickly and there is not much description.

### Language focus

1)

| | What happens |
|---|---|
| Beginning | Introduced to Red Riding Hood and how she plans to visit grandmother. |
| Middle | Introduced the Big Bad Wolf and how he plans to eat her. |
| Top | We don't know. |

2) *Own answers*

### Links to writing

1), 2) *Own answers*

## 19 Time and place: drawing inferences

### Comprehension

1) Dad says, *'It's your first time out.'*
2) The boy looks lost and the bushes are thicker.
3) summer
4) The amount of light in the sky.
5) The pictures help us.
6) The story shows the progression of one day from morning to evening.

### Language focus

1)

| Picture | The place | The time |
|---|---|---|
| 1 | his house – outside | early morning |
| 2 | open countryside | late morning |
| 3 | edge of wood | midday |
| 4 | in the woods | twilight |
| 5 | in a puddle | early evening |
| 6 | home | late evening |

2), 3) *Own answers*

### Links to writing

1), 2) *Own answers*

## 20 Paragraphs 1

### Comprehension

1) A short tale to teach a moral lesson, often using personified animals or inanimate objects as the main characters.
2) Yes, this fable uses the Sun and Wind as the main characters. The Sun *'smiled'*. *'The Wind thought he was more powerful.'*
3) They were deciding who was strongest.
4) The Sun is *'all fire'* and *'can destroy anything'* it wants. The Wind is *'all strength and force'*.
5) Who can make a man take his coat off fastest.
6) The Wind *'blew and blew'* trying *'to tear the coat from the man's back'*. The Sun *'shone down on the man'* and won the challenge.

## Comprehension

1) From where does Mr Croc get the idea to do some exercise?

2) What three kinds of exercises does he do?

3) How does he realise that he should not eat before exercising?

4) How does the reader know that time has passed?

5) Why are people looking strangely at him at the end of the story?

6) What do you think the joke is behind the cartoon story?

## Language focus

1) Make a chart of the order of events in the story.

| Event | Time in story | What happens |
|-------|---------------|--------------|
| 1     |               |              |
| 2     |               |              |

2) Tell the story with the events in a different order. What happens? Decide if there is a correct order to the events in this story. Explain why.

3) Write the events in paragraphs. How will you decide what goes in each paragraph? Think about a new paragraph for each new big idea.

4) If you were writing the story, which of these connectives would you use to show the right order?

**first     then     because     while     before     after     although**

## Links to writing

1) Draw another cartoon story about Mr Croc and what he gets up to. Use speech bubbles. Fit the whole story on to one page. Decide upon the correct order for your story. What comes first? What comes next? How does the story end?

2) Now write the story. You will need to use a new paragraph for each big idea or theme.

   **You could just say what happens in the beginning, middle and end – three paragraphs.**

   **You could build up the story. What is the problem?**

   **Who are the characters? What are they like?**

   **How do they solve the problem?**

# 16 Planning your writing: problem solving

Let's look at a very strange story to see how it is planned.

From *Soupy Boy*

**On a visit to a soup factory with his parents, he fell into a vat of tomato soup!**

**Into the soup the daring diver dove. HOWEVER, this wasn't just any old soup, oh no! Unknown to all, this soup was infected by RADIOACTIVE COSMIC DUST! And so, by the time Ashley was fished out, he'd mutated into...**

*Damon Burnard*

## Speak about it

Why is it important to plan your stories before you write them?
What would happen if you didn't plan your stories?
What might a plan for your story look like?
Is it important to have a beginning? A middle? An end? Why?

## Comprehension

1) Where was the hero of our story visiting when the accident happened? What was he called?

2) What happened to him there?

3) Who volunteers to rescue the boy?

4) Why was the soup dangerous?

5) Why do you think some words are written in capital letters in a different typeface?

6) What do the last three dots on the page tell you about the story?

## Language focus

1) Look at the title of the story. Write about what you think will be in this story, e.g. *superhero*, *fighting villain*, *disguise*, etc.

2) How is this story planned? Copy and complete the chart to help.

| Beginning | |
| --- | --- |
| Middle | |
| End | We don't know! |

3) Look at what you are told in this unit about the story. Make notes on:

   **a.** opening      **b.** characters      **c.** problem

4) Now make notes about what you think will happen in the rest of the story.

   **a.** dealing with problem      **b.** solving the problem      **c.** the end

## Links to writing

1) Write the story after the passage ends.

   **Use drawings and speech bubbles.**

   **Use a computer to change important words into different typefaces.**

2) Write a story of your own child superhero.

   **What will he or she be called?**

   **What will the plan of your story be like?**

# 17 Capturing imagination – words and phrases

**Different kinds of words that you use help to make a picture in your reader's mind. Let's look at some of these.**

### From *Charmed Life*

The door of the room sprang open of its own accord and the **huge** spider went silently creeping towards it, swaying on its **hairy** legs. It squeezed its legs inward to get through the door, and crept onwards, down the passage beyond.

Gwendolen touched the other creatures, one by one. The earwigs lumbered up and off, like **shiny horned** cows, **bright brown** and glistening. The frogs rose up, as big as men, and walked flap, flop on their **enormous** feet, and with their arms trailing like gorillas. Their **mottled** skin quivered, and little holes kept opening and shutting. The **puffy** place under their chins made gulping movements. The black beetle crawled on branched legs, such a **big, black** slab that it could barely get through the door. Cat could see it, and all the others, going in **slow, silent** procession down the **grass-green, glowing** corridor.

*Diana Wynne Jones*

## Speak about it

What is an **adjective**? Look at the words in bold.
What is a **verb**?
Why is it important to use descriptive words in your writing?
What would your writing be like if you didn't? How would your audience react?

## Comprehension

1) How do you know the door of the room opened fast?

2) What came through it? How did it move?

3) Which words tell you it was so large that it was a tight fit?

4) What do the earwigs remind the author of?

5) What was surprising about the size of the frogs? Find some evidence.

6) Explain how all these creatures moved down the corridor.

## Language focus

1) Read the extract aloud without the adjectives in bold. What difference does it make?

2) Write some of your own adjectives, e.g.: **a *huge* spider** – **a *large* spider** – **an *enormous* spider** – **a *hairy* spider**. Talk about how each adjective says something different to the reader's imagination.

3) Find the adverbs used in the passage. What do they add that is extra to the description? If you took them away, would it make a difference?

4) 'Flap, flop' describes the sound made by the frogs. You can hear it because of the words. Write sentences using your own sound words to describe:

   a. the breaking of a window

   b. moving water in a washing machine

   c. leaves on a tree blowing in the wind

## Links to writing

1) Continue the story. Write about what happens next. What will the creatures do? Will Gwendolen change them back? How will the story end?

   **Use words to help you make the scene come alive.**

   **Which of your senses will be involved? Use sound words.**

   **Choose adjectives and adverbs carefully.**

   **Use vivid verbs – not boring ones. Look in a thesaurus.**

2) Imagine that you are a wizard or a witch. One of your spells goes wrong. Write a story about what happens.

# 18  Predicting what might happen

**Can you tell what might happen at the end of a story?**

**Big Bad Raps**

Just on the edge
of a deep, dark wood
lived a girl called
Little Red Riding Hood.
Her grandmother lived
not far away,
so Red went to pay her a
visit one day …

And the Big Bad Wolf,
who knew her plan
he turned his nose
and ran and ran.
He ran till he came
to her grandmother's door.

Then he locked her up
with a great big roar.
He took her place
in her nice warm bed,
and he waited there
for Little Miss Red.

*Tony Mitton*

**Speak about it**

You probably know this story – what is it?
How do you predict that it will end?
Does a story always have to have a 'happily ever after' ending?
How else can stories end?

## Comprehension

1) What traditional story does this poem use?

2) Which characters are in it? Are they behaving in the way you would expect? Explain why.

3) Explain what happens in the traditional story as you know it.

4) What is a **rap**? What features do you expect a rap to have?

5) Does this poem contain these features? Explain how.

6) How is this version of the traditional story different?

## Language focus

1) Copy and complete the chart to say what happens in each part of the story.

| | What happens? |
| --- | --- |
| Beginning | |
| Middle | |
| End | We don't know. |

2) Do you know the ending of the story? What details in the poem tell you that it might not end happily? Use a chart to collect information.

| | Words in the poem | What they tell me |
| --- | --- | --- |
| the wood | | |
| the wolf | | |

## Links to writing

1) Continue this story, but not in poetry. Give it a 'happily ever after' ending for young children. Then write another ending, but more bloodthirsty, for children of your age. Would this still be 'happily ever after'?

   **How will you make sure your story follows steps, so your reader can understand the end?**

   **How will you make time pass?**

   **How will you make the story exciting, but not give too much away?**

2) Choose another fairy story or traditional tale. Write the story, but give it a very different ending.

# 19 Time and place: drawing inferences

## Speak about it

How can you tell how the characters feel from the words in the cartoon?

How can you tell what is happening from the pictures?

How can you tell where the story is set, the time of day and the time of year?

Do all stories do this?

## Comprehension

1) How do you know the boy has not been out on his bike before?

2) When he gets to the countryside, how do you guess that he is lost?

3) At what time of the year is this story set?

4) How do we know what time of day it is in each picture?

5) There are few words in this story. How do we know what happens to the boy?

6) How do you know that time has passed in this story?

## Language focus

1) Look at each picture. Using a chart like this one, explain what each picture tells us about the place and the time.

| Picture | The place | The time |
|---------|-----------|----------|
| 1 | his house – outside | early morning |

2) The story is set in the countryside. Write a list of words to describe it. Use a chart about your senses to help.

| Seeing | Hearing | Touching | Smelling | Tasting |
|--------|---------|----------|----------|---------|
| | birds singing | | flowers | |

3) List the detail in the passage about the place.

| Picture | What it tells me | Which senses does it appeal to? Why? | How does it make me feel? |
|---------|------------------|--------------------------------------|---------------------------|
| dark clouds – thunder and lightning | storm | hearing, seeing, can feel the rain | scared, frightened |

## Links to writing

1) Now turn the cartoon into a story in paragraphs. You could write one paragraph for each picture.

2) Write a description of your school and its playground at lunchtime. Start with quiet. Then make it noisy and busy. Go back to silent again.

   **Make notes about what you can see, feel, hear, taste and touch.**

   **Describe the details of what the place looks like.**

   **What will the weather be like? This will make a difference to your senses.**

   **How will you show time passing?**

# 20 Paragraphs 1

### *The Sun and the Wind*

It was not a happy day in Ancient Greece. The Sun and the Wind were having an argument. People on the ground were scared. They could not get on with their farming. The Sun and the Wind were deciding who was the strongest.

'I am the most powerful,' said the Sun. 'I am all fire. I can destroy anything I want.' He pointed a few rays at a tree. It burst into flames. He smiled. The people hid.

The Wind thought he was more powerful. 'I am all strength and force,' he said. He blew gently. The people smiled as the leaves rustled. He blew strongly and a tree fell to the ground. People ran and hid. The wind smiled.

A farmer on the ground was tired of this. He shouted up, 'Why don't you have one last challenge to prove who is the strongest? At least the people of the Earth would then be safe.'

The Sun and the Wind stared each other out. After a time, they knew they must agree. A small, dark man walked by. They decided to use him as a test. 'Whoever can make him take off his coat the fastest will win,' said the Sun.

So, the Wind blew and blew. He tried to tear the coat from the man's back. But the man just hugged the coat to himself even more and struggled on.

The Sun decided to be gentle in his approach. He shone down on the man. Suddenly the man started to become very hot. He puffed and panted. He sweated. So what did he do? He took off his coat.

The Sun had won the battle. But what is the moral of this story? The Sun won the challenge not by being fierce and violent, but by being gentle and persistent. You could try that as well.

*Aesop*

### Speak about it

What is a **paragraph**?
Why is it important to write in paragraphs?
What would happen if you didn't?
How do you know when to start a new paragraph?

## Comprehension

1) What is a **fable**? What feature should a fable always have?

2) Does this fable have this? Find the evidence.

3) What was the argument between the Sun and the Wind about?

4) Explain why each of them thought they were the most powerful.

5) What test did they set?

6) What did each of them try to do to win?

## Language focus

1) Make notes about what detail is in each paragraph. A chart might help.

| Paragraph | Detail in it |
|-----------|--------------|
| 1 | The main characters. They have an argument. |

2) Is every paragraph about something different? Write a rule about when you should use a new paragraph.

3) Here is another one of Aesop's fables. Write it out correctly in paragraphs, following your rule. Talk with others about whether they have something different and why.

   **A crow was dying of thirst. He saw a big jug of water on the ground. When he came up to it, there was only a little water in the bottom. He tried to overturn the jug, but it was too heavy. At last he saw some small stones. He threw them into the jug until the water level rose. He then drank to his heart's content. This proves that if you are clever you will be successful in the end.**

## Links to writing

1) Here are some notes about another fable called *The Fox and the Crow*. Use these notes. Follow the events in order to write clear paragraphs. Add details to make an atmosphere. Don't forget the setting! What's the moral of the story?

   **crow → stole piece of cheese → flew into tree → cheese in beak → fox came by → hungry → spoke to crow → no cheese → flattered crow → said had nice voice → said was beautiful → crow sang → cheese fell out of beak to ground → fox ran away with it → may have been beautiful → no brains!**

# 21 Test your grammar, punctuation and spelling

## Grammar

### Using prepositions to express time and cause

Choose a preposition to fill the gap. These words may help you: *before, after, during, in, because, of.*

1) _____ my lunch break, I chat with my friends.

2) We are not allowed to eat our snack _____ playtime.

3) We feel rested _____ the summer holidays.

4) We have to stay behind at lunchtime _____ we were chatting too much.

5) _____ tricky lessons we can work with a friend.

6) It's home time _____ ten minutes; hooray!

### Word families

Copy and complete the chart.

| Base word | Word 1 – adjective | Word 2 – noun | Word 3 – adverb |
|---|---|---|---|
| *music* | *musical* | *musician* | *musically* |
| science | | | |
| mathematics | | | |
| history | | | |
| art | | | |
| geography | | | |

## Punctuation

### Contractions
Write the long form(s) of each of these.

Example  He's → He is

1) I'm
2) doesn't
3) won't
4) didn't
5) might've
6) should've
7) it's
8) can't

## Spelling

### Words with endings sounding like /zhuh/ or /chuh/
Write the correct ending.

Example  We have to mea_sure_ the playground with the tape.

1) We are on a desert island looking for the trea_____.
2) The furni_____ will not fit in the room.
3) The dragon was a fearsome crea_____.
4) I take a great pic_____ with my camera.
5) I love to lick the cake mix_____ bowl.

### Root words ending in -tch or -ch plus -er
Add the correct letters **-tch** or **-ch** to complete these words.

1) We love our tea_____er.
2) When I went to hospital they put me on the stre_____er.
3) We would all like to be ri_____er.
4) I'm not very good at kicking but I am a good ca_____er.
5) We buy our meat from the local bu_____er.
6) I'm on the lookout; I'm the wa_____er.

# 22  Paragraphs 2

Jamie has written all about his visit to the British Museum. Has he used paragraphs correctly?

**We went on a school visit to the British Museum.** The reason is because we are learning about invaders and settlers in history. People who invaded Britain and then lived here were the Romans, the Anglo-Saxons and the Vikings.

**First we went to see the rooms about Vikings.** They came in the 8th century AD until around 1100. Vikings were warriors. People were scared of them.

> This is the topic sentence. It tells us what the paragraph will be about.

**Then we went to see the Romans.** They came to Britain in AD 43. Boudicca fought the Romans but lost. She was killed.

> Connectives (in red) tell us about how to order paragraphs.

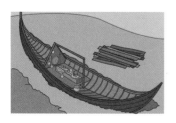

**After that we went to see the Anglo-Saxon Sutton Hoo ship burial.** They found lots of treasure from the 7th century AD there.

> The sentences tell us more about the topic sentence.

**I learned a lot from my visit to the British Museum.** The best thing I learned was that Vikings didn't really wear helmets with horns like they do in the films. I also learned that the Roman soldiers didn't like it here. It was too cold for them. Finally, I found out that Anglo-Saxon words are still here in place names.

## Speak about it

What is a **paragraph**?
What is a **topic sentence**?
Why are they important to your reader?
How do you know when to start a new paragraph?
What other words show you the correct order of the paragraphs?

## Comprehension

1) Why did Jamie visit the British Museum?

2) Which people invaded Britain and lived here?

3) When did the Vikings come to Britain?

4) Who fought the Romans? What happened to her?

5) List two things that Jamie learned from his visit.

6) Do you think Jamie has used paragraphs correctly? Say why.

## Language focus

1) Explain how the topic sentences, in bold, tell you what else is going to be in the paragraph.

2) These sentences are about making toast. They are not in the right order. Put them in the right order. Write the paragraph. Which is your topic sentence? How do you know?

| |
| --- |
| Before you can switch it on, you need to push down the handle so the bread goes into the toaster. |
| Place some bread in the slots in the toaster. |
| You'll need to turn the dial on the toaster to the right time. |
| When the toast is ready, it will pop up. |
| Switch it on. |
| To make toast with a toaster is very easy. |

## Links to writing

1) Here is a plan for a piece of writing: My favourite TV programme.

| | |
| --- | --- |
| Paragraph 1 | The sorts of programmes I like and why |
| Paragraph 2 | My favourite programme and what it's about |
| Paragraph 3 | Characters – who I like and don't like – and why |
| Paragraph 4 | My favourite episode |
| Paragraph 5 | Why it's better than others – why it's different |

Write the first sentence for each paragraph.

2) Choose one paragraph. Write the paragraph under your topic sentence.

# 23 Punctuation of direct speech

**Can you decide how and when to punctuate speech?**

**Alice travels to a magical world through a mirror and meets a very rude Humpty Dumpty.**

**Adapted from *Through the Looking Glass***

"Don't stand chattering to yourself like that," Humpty Dumpty said, looking at her for the first time, "but tell me your name and your business."

"My name is Alice, but …"

"It's a stupid name!" Humpty Dumpty interrupted impatiently. "What does it mean?"

"Must a name mean something?" Alice asked doubtfully. "Don't you think you would be safer on the ground than on a wall? You will fall off."

"Why, if ever I did fall off – which there is no chance of – but if I did …" Here Humpty looked very grandly at Alice. "If I did fall, then the King has promised me – with his very own mouth – to…"

"I know," said Alice. "To send all his horses and his men to put you back together again."

"Now I declare, that's too bad!" Humpty Dumpty cried. "You've been listening at doors or you couldn't have known!"

"I haven't indeed," Alice replied very gently. "It's in a book."

*Lewis Carroll*

**Speak about it**

Why is it important to use the correct punctuation when you write someone's words?

How is it different from other punctuation?

Which words do you put inside these punctuation marks?

What rules do you know about punctuating speech?

## Comprehension

**1)** How do you think that Humpty Dumpty is rude? Give an example.

**2)** Where does Alice find him sitting?

**3)** What does she think will be safer for him? Why?

**4)** Alice knows his story. How does he think she found out?

**5)** How did Alice (and you) know about what happens to Humpty Dumpty?

## Language focus

**1)** Write three examples of speech in the passage. Underline the words inside speech marks.

**2)** Put the correct words in inverted commas (speech marks) and write each sentence correctly.

    **a.** Fred said, I feel happy today.

    **b.** My team didn't win again, sighed Ranjit.

    **c.** Have you ever been to Australia, asked Tracy.

**3)** Look at these examples. Find where the punctuation is wrong and correct them.

    **a.** "I want a drink" said Tracy

    **b.** "How many sweets have you taken" asked Fred

    **c.** "That's not fair if you've got more money" said Harry

## Links to writing

**1)** Draw a cartoon story of Alice meeting Humpty Dumpty. Use speech bubbles. Include what you know happens afterwards.

**2)** Write this passage out and punctuate it correctly. Underline the words the characters say before you start. Remember to put each new speaker on a new line.

**two men had just won the lottery I feel a bit hungry I'll buy some pies said one that's great said the other as they were eating their pies they passed a motor showroom I've always wanted a Rolls Royce said one I'll buy a couple said his friend no said the first man these are on me you bought the pies**

# 24 Using connectives

**Can you decide *how* and *when* to use connectives?**

| One piece of information | This connective just **joins** one piece of information to another. | Another piece of information |

The car was going very fast AND I didn't see it.

| One piece of information | This connective says that something else was possible. It **adds** information. | Extra information |

It was heading straight for me ALTHOUGH he didn't realise I was fast on my bike.

| One piece of information | This connective gives us **a reason** for something. | This is the reason for, or the result of, the first piece of information. |

I think I am alive today BECAUSE I went to road safety lessons.

Cycling is fun **and** it is healthy. School work can keep you busy **but** we want you to spend more time pedalling, **and** less time sitting in front of the computer. Our site lists useful bike stuff on the Internet **because** it's often hard to find what you want. It's easy to find the information out there **when** someone helps you. It's free and it's interesting **so** why aren't you finding out more?

www.bikeforall.net

### Speak about it

What is a **connective**?
What do connectives connect?
What kind of words are connectives?
What would happen in sentences if you did not use them?

## Comprehension

1) Which words do you not understand? Look them up in a dictionary.

2) Give one reason why cycling is good for you.

3) What does the writer really mean when she says 'more time pedalling'?

4) What does she think young people spend most of their time doing?

5) What is on their Internet site?

6) Why might it be useful?

## Language focus

1) Read the passage without the connectives. What difference does it make? What do connectives do in sentences?

2) Make these pairs of sentences into one sentence. Choose the best connective.

    **a.** She put up her umbrella. It was raining. **when but because**

    **b.** The gold medal was hard to win. He was the obvious winner.
    **after if although**

    **c.** I hurt my arm. I was playing rugby. **after while and**

## Links to writing

1) Choose connectives from the box to go in these gaps. Compare your answers with a friend. Do different connectives make the sentences mean something different?

    **a.** He slept through the show … he missed the end.

    **b.** You will get no pocket money … you begin to tidy your bedroom.

    **c.** I liked the story of the film … the acting was dreadful.

    **d.** She worked hard for a term … she came top in the exams.

    **e.** You only stand a chance to win … you buy a lottery ticket.

| if | when |
|---|---|
| because | |
| although | after |
| while | before |
| so | unless |

# 25 Clauses

### From 'The First Stamps'

The world's first postage stamps were issued by Great Britain on May 1, 1840, and came into use on May 6. Their introduction was due to the efforts of Rowland Hill, at one time a Birmingham schoolmaster, who produced a plan to reform the Post Office. He succeeded in interesting Parliament in his plan, which was adopted in 1839.

Before 1840 the postage on a letter was usually paid by the person who received it, and as the postal rates were very high, some people, especially the very poor, used to dread a visit from the postman. Postage was charged according to the distance a letter had to travel and its weight: a letter weighing two ounces, sent from London to Croydon, cost two shillings and four pence.

The high charges were caused by inefficient working of the Post Office, and Rowland Hill's plan showed that letters could be sent all over the country for one penny each, and still enable the Post Office to make a good profit. So as to make the sender of a letter responsible for the postage, Hill suggested that it should be paid in advance, by sticking the stamp on the letter.

There were two values of stamps: a one-penny black and a two-penny blue, both showing the head of Queen Victoria. They were printed in London in sheets of 240 stamps, and were imperforate (having no perforations). Although over 100 years old the Penny Black and Twopenny Blue are not very rare, but are in great demand by collectors.

Two years after Britain had introduced postage stamps to the world, a private postal service, working in New York, issued a stamp, the first to appear in the Western hemisphere.

*L N and M Williams*

## Speak about it

What is a **clause**? Can you find examples in the passage?
How are they different from **phrases**?
Are clauses complete sentences?
What job do clauses perform?

**Comprehension**

1) When did postage stamps come into use in Britain?

2) What had been Rowland Hill's previous profession?

3) Explain how the postal service worked before Rowland Hill changed things.

4) Why did poor people not like this system?

5) How was the new system different?

6) What was special about the first sheets of stamps produced?

7) What words tell you that the postal service in the USA was not run by the government?

 **Language focus**

1) There are three main ways to add a clause to a sentence: at the beginning, in the middle, and at the end. Try to find an example of each in the text.

2) Add clauses beginning with **because** or **if** to these sentences.

   **a.** We will not be going to the circus this evening …

   **b.** My nose turned a bright red colour …

   **c.** I decided to buy the trainers …

   Make up five more examples of your own.

3) Now change around the sentence structure. Start each sentence with the **Because** or **If** clause. What difference do you notice?

 **Links to writing**

1) **The flashy car got out of control** when **I went too fast**. → When **I went too fast, the flashy car got out of control**.

   Write five more examples of sentences using clauses beginning with **When**. Use the clauses at the beginning and ending of sentences to experiment with the structure of sentences. What difference does it make?

2) Write five sentences each using clauses beginning with **Until** and **Although**.

# 26 Choosing the best vocabulary and grammar – adjectives

Let's investigate *how* and *when* to use adjectives when writing sentences.

**From *Josie Smith at Christmas***

Josie Smith ate her breakfast as fast as she could and then she put her coat and wellingtons on and her **itchy** scarf and went out in the yard.

The snow in the yard was **thick** and **soft** and the **knobbly black** stones of the walls had **little** slices of snow in all their cracks. Josie Smith poked her finger into the **clean** snow and tasted some. Then she made some footprints right across the middle and walked back in them and made them go back to front. Then she stood still with her face to the sky. The snowflakes were twirling round and round and round and round right up as far as the top of the sky and they made Josie Smith feel dizzy. She shut her eyes and let the **big** snowflakes land on her face and tickle and burn and melt. It was very quiet. She pulled her tongue out and a snowflake melted there.

*Magdalen Nabb*

## Speak about it

What is an **adjective**?
What kind of word do they describe?
Why is it important to use them in your writing?
What would happen to your reader's interest if you did not use them?

## Comprehension

1) Why do you think Josie ate her breakfast so fast?

2) Why might she not have liked wearing her scarf?

3) Write down two adjectives that the author uses to describe the snow.

4) What did Josie do to taste the snow?

5) Explain what she did with her footprints. Why do you think she did this?

6) When she looked at the snow falling, how did this make her feel?

## Language focus

1) Write out some sentences without the adjectives, e.g. 'Josie *put on her scarf*'. What difference does it make? What information is left out?

2) Add two or three adjectives to the nouns in these boring sentences, e.g. '*The man walked down the road.*' → '*The tall, thin man walked down the long, dark road.*'

   a. The girls pushed the car.

   b. The boy cleaned his shoes.

   c. The elephant ran through the jungle.

   d. He put on a clean shirt.

3) **Nice** is an overused adjective. Think of adjectives that you could use instead of **nice** that would have the same meaning. Write the sentences.

   a. a nice jacket      b. a nice cottage      c. a nice meal

   d. a nice film        e. a nice holiday      f. a nice dog

## Links to writing

1) Continue Josie's description of being in the snow. What did she do next? What was it like? Use adjectives to describe what she feels, sees, touches, tastes and hears.

2) Collect adjectives under these headings to describe: a fox, a tortoise, a lion, a snake, an owl.

| Shape | Size | Colour | Texture |
|-------|------|--------|---------|
|       |      |        |         |

Write sentences containing some of these adjectives.

# 27 Choosing the best vocabulary and grammar – adverbs and prepositions

Let's investigate how and when to use verbs and prepositions in your writing. Prepositions tell you about the position of something or somebody, e.g. the man sat <u>under</u> an umbrella <u>on</u> the beach <u>by</u> the sea.

**From *The Gigantic Badness***

He lived over the hill behind the town, but sometimes he crossed the field where the saw-mill was and if the smoke was coming out of the tall chimney he leaned <u>over</u> and blew <u>down</u> it so that the men who were working in the mill coughed and spluttered.

Sometimes in the early morning he reached a finger to the schoolhouse bell hanging high against the roof, and all the children, halfway through their breakfasts, gulped and gobbled and raced into school half an hour early. Once when Tom was sailing his boats in the river the Giant decided it was a good day to take a swim farther upstream, and he enjoyed it so much that he lay on his back, kicking and splashing. Water rose up round him in fountains, and then poured downstream in great waves, so that Tom's boats were swamped, and those that didn't sink were tossed against the bank with their rigging tangled and the thin stick masts smashed into pieces. That was bad enough, but a week later while Tom was out on the hill flying his new kite the Giant walked by, tangling the string of the kite in his bootlaces so that the kite came down in the middle of a gorse bush, all torn and broken.

*Janet McNeill*

**Speak about it**

What is an adverb? Look at the underlined words.
What is a preposition? Find some in the passage.
Can you write sentences without them? Give examples.

## Comprehension

1) Where did the Giant live?
2) What did he do at the mill? Why would this have been unpopular?
3) What did he do at the school? Do you think the children would have liked this? Explain why.
4) Why was Tom so annoyed with the Giant when he played with his boats?
5) How does the author give you a sense of how big the Giant is compared to Tom? Where does it tell you this?

## Language focus

1) Choose a preposition from the box. Complete the sentences:

   before   after
   beside
   through   down
   across   beneath
   with   under

   a. Deep _____ the earth lived a huge dragon.
   b. I found the secret map ____ a large pile of paper.
   c. The beetle scuttled _____ the table in front of me.
   d. I ran _____ the ball, but it rolled in the river.

2) Write new sentences using the remaining prepositions. Then see if you can give them different meanings by changing the preposition, e.g. the cat sat **on** the mat, **under** the mat, **by** the mat.

3) Make the verbs in these phrases more exciting, e.g. **coming** could be **puffing**, **pouring**, **gushing**.

   a. the smoke was **coming** out of the tall chimney      b. **blew** down it
   c. the Giant **decided** it was a good day

   Find adverbs to describe these verbs, e.g.: **smoke pouring** *dangerously*.

4) Most adverbs end in **-ly**, but not all. Write the examples from the passage. Find other examples and use them in sentences with the verbs **shouted**, **whispered** and **argued**.

## Links to writing

1) Write about how Tom got his revenge against the Giant. Make the story more exciting by using vivid verbs, adverbs and prepositions.
   **What happened to make Tom really mad? Describe this.**
   **What did he decide to do? How did he do it?**

# 28 Test your grammar, punctuation and spelling

## The perfect form of verbs

Rewrite each phrase using the perfect form.

| The past tense: *Last week...* | The present perfect: *...this morning* |
| --- | --- |
| I jumped | I have jumped |
| I ran | |
| He kicked | |
| She threw | |
| We cheered | |
| They scored | |

## What is it?

conjunction

adverb

preposition

prefix

consonant

vowel

Each question below has something <u>underlined</u>. Choose a word from the list above to describe each <u>underlined</u> section.

Example    A dog slept <u>under</u> the bridge.
           <u>Under</u> is a preposition.

1) <u>b</u>  <u>z</u>  <u>t</u>

2) The dog barked <u>noisily</u>.

3) <u>a</u>  <u>u</u>  <u>e</u>

4) The swan glided <u>smoothly</u>.

5) She fell <u>on</u> her nose.

6) It was all a <u>mis</u>understanding.

7) We wanted to take part <u>because</u> it was important.

8) <u>While</u> we ran they cheered.

9) We went to see the <u>super</u>star.

## Punctuation

### Inverted commas (speech marks)

Add the inverted commas (speech marks) to these sentences.

1) I looked up and shouted get me out of here!
2) She smiled at me and said will you be my friend?
3) The dog barked at me when I said here boy!
4) You can never tell with animals she yelled but trust me this one is safe.
5) Are you coming with me or not she asked.
6) If you are in yellow group she shouted stand with me.

## Spelling

### Adding prefixes

Join a prefix from the left column to a root word in the right column and write the complete word.

Make spelling adjustments to the prefix if you need to.

| Prefix | Root word |
| --- | --- |
| inter- | hero |
| dis- | behave |
| super- | appear |
| mis- | graph |
| auto- | act |
| im- | legible |
| ir- | possible |
| il- | regular |

### Useful words

Choose the correct word and write it.

1) The situation is very (peculiar/particular).
2) You (decide/describe) what we did yesterday in the playground.
3) When swimming you have to learn to (breathe/breath) well.
4) I (thought/through) it was a good idea.
5) Famous people often have a body (guard/guide).
6) The teacher said we had a (surprise/suppose).

# Glossary

**adjective**   often called a 'describing' word but it makes the meaning of a noun clearer, e.g. The girl did **good** work, or is used after the verb *to be*, e.g. Her test result was **excellent**

**adverb**   a word that makes the meanings of verbs, adjectives or other adverbs more specific; often they describe how or when something happens. For examples see Unit 27

**apostrophe**   a punctuation mark that can show the place of a missing letter, e.g. **I'm**, or can show possession, e.g. **Evie's** mum

**clause**   a special type of phrase, which has a verb in it that describes what is happening. For examples see Unit 25

**comma**   a punctuation mark that marks a slight break between different parts of a sentence. Used properly, commas make the meaning of sentences clear by grouping and separating words, phrases and clauses. Mainly used in lists, in direct speech, to separate clauses and to mark off certain parts of a sentence

**conjunction**   a conjunction links two words or phrases together, e.g. **and, when**

**connective**   words that join parts of sentences together

**consonant letter**   these are *b, c, d, f, g, h, j, k, l, m, n, p, q, r, s, t, v, w, x, y, z*

**determiner**   words that are used with nouns to make the noun more clear

**direct speech**   the actual words spoken by someone and reported to the reader inside inverted commas or speech marks. The opposite of reported speech

**homograph**   Different words that are spelled the same but pronounced differently, e.g. **bow/bow**

**homophone**   Different words that sound the same but are spelled differently, e.g. **hear/here**

**inverted commas**   inverted commas can be single – 'g' – or double – "g". They are also known as quotation marks, speech marks or quotes. Usually used to mark the beginning and end of direct speech

**noun**   a word (often a person, place or thing) which can be singular or plural and is the subject to go with the verb

**phrase**   a group of words that are connected grammatically, usually because all the words help to clarify or change the main word of the phrase. If the main word is a verb, the phrase becomes a clause or a sentence

**prefix**   added to the beginning of a word to turn it into another word. For examples see Unit 12

**preposition**   a word that links a noun or pronoun to some other word in the sentence, e.g. **in, since**

**simile**   a figure of speech that says that one thing is like another, different thing. We can use similes to make descriptions more emphatic or vivid

**subordinate clause**    a clause that depends on a main clause for its meaning. Together with a main clause, a subordinate clause forms part of a longer sentence. A sentence may contain more than one subordinate clause

**suffix**    added to the end of a word to turn it into another word.  It can change the function of the word too, e.g. **terror** (noun) – **terrorise** (verb). For examples see Units 1, 2 and 11

**tense**    the choice between verb forms, often to tell us when something happened. Present tense is about the present or sometimes the future (**may**, **intend**, **plan**, **will**) and the past tense tells us that something happened in the past. For examples see Units 3 and 15

**verb**    every verb has a tense and often tells us about the action of a person or thing

**vowel letter**    these are *a, e, i, o, u* and sometimes *y*

**word family**    the words in a word family are normally linked to each other by a form, grammar and meaning, e.g. **plumber** – **plumb** or **defensive** – **defend** – **defence**

## Punctuation chart

| Punctuation mark word | Symbol | Note | Example |
|---|---|---|---|
| apostrophe | ' | Can show that something belongs to someone or something<br><br>Can show that letters are missed out | the girl's hat<br>the girls' hats<br><br>can't  cannot<br>she'd  she would/she had |
| brackets | ( ) | Can be used to show that a word or phrase has been added | We said thank you (but we didn't mean it really!). |
| bullet point | • | Can be used to make a list clear | Things to buy:<br>• sausages<br>• bananas<br>• baked beans |
| colon | : | Can be used before you make a list<br>Can be used to give more examples after the first part of a sentence | See above<br><br>The dogs are very funny: they are trained to do tricks. |
| comma | , | Can make a sentence clear or change the meaning of the sentence<br><br>To separate the items in a list | Slow children crossing.<br>Slow, children crossing.<br><br>I like sausages, bananas and baked beans. |
| dash | – | Can be used to add a bit more information to a sentence<br>It's informal | The dogs are very funny – the old brown one makes me laugh. |
| full stop | . | Can be used at the end of a sentence to show it has finished<br>It also shows that a word is shortened or contracted | I went to the dog show.<br><br>On the 23rd of Sept. I went to the dog show. |

# Handy hints

## Spelling

### Top tips on spelling

1) Try using your phonics knowledge first.

2) Does it look right? If not, what changes would make sense? Do you know another way of writing the sound for the bit that looks wrong?

3) Do you know another word that sounds similar and that you could use as a starting point, e.g. if it's **baby/babies**, then it's probably going to be **city/cities**.

4) If it's a long word, say the syllables; write each syllable as a chunk.

5) Think about the root word and then about whether the word might have a prefix or a suffix that might help you to spell it, e.g. **understand, misunderstand, misunderstanding**.

6) Think about word families: **teach, teacher, teaching** or **photograph, photography, photosynthesis**.

7) Don't always rely on the spellcheck when working on the computer – keep thinking for yourself so that when you are writing away from technology or on your own, you don't get stuck.

## Vocabulary

### Top tips on vocabulary

1) Don't keep using the same words over and over again because it makes your writing very dull.

2) Every time you want to use **said**, try to think of a different verb to make it more interesting for your reader.

3) Don't use **okay, great, nice, really** and **boring** in your writing.

4) Don't avoid using interesting words just because you aren't sure of the spelling – just have a try!

## Commonly misspelled words

| | | | | |
|---|---|---|---|---|
| accident(ally) | continue | group | natural | recent |
| address | describe | guide | notice | reign |
| appear | difficult | heart | often | sentence |
| believe | early | history | ordinary | special |
| breath | eight/eighth | increase | peculiar | strange |
| build | exercise | interest | popular | suppose |
| calendar | experiment | knowledge | possess(ion) | therefore |
| centre | famous | length | potatoes | thought |
| certain | February | material | probably | various |
| complete | fruit | mention | purpose | woman |

## Presentation

### Top tips on handwriting

1) Make sure that your pen or pencil is comfortable (and that the pencil is sharp).

2) Use an eraser (rubber) if you make a mistake.

3) If **you** can't read it then others won't be able to!

4) Try to keep it neat all the time.

### And …

Use capital letters for:

- people's names

- people's titles (like **Mrs** Jones)

- places

- days of the week

- months of the year

### And …

Use a full stop at the end of a sentence unless you are using a **?** or a **!**

63

Rising Stars UK Ltd, 7 Hatchers Mews, Bermondsey Street, London SE1 3GS

www.risingstars-uk.com

**Acknowledgements**

Page 10 – Photograph by Wig Worland © Wig Worland

Page 12 – From The Girl Who Stayed for Half a Week by Gene Kemp, from Roundabout, Faber and Faber 1993

Page 22 – Leaflet: Rutland Water Butterfly Farm

Page 28 – 'Ten White Snowmen' by John Foster

Page 32 – 'Mr Croc Gets Fit' by Frank Rogers from *Mr Croc*, A&C Black

Page 34 – Extract from *Soupy Boy*, by Damon Burnard, Corgi Yearling Books, Transworld

Page 36 – Extract from *Charmed Life* by Diana Wynne Jones, Macmillan and Puffin 1979, © Dianna Wynne Jones, 1977. Permission granted by the author

Page 38 – 'Big Bad Raps' by Tony Mitton, Orchard Books

Page 52 – Adapted extract from *Postage Stamps* by L.N and M. Williams, Puffin Picture Books, 1950. Reprinted by permission of Mrs D Williams

Page 54 – From *Josie Smith at Christmas* by Magdalen Nabb, Collins Children's Books

Page 56 – 'The Gigantic Badness' by Janet McNeill, from *Bad Boys*, ed Eileen Colwell, Puffin 1972

Every effort has been made to trace copyright holders and obtain their permission for the use of copyright materials. The authors and publisher will gladly receive information enabling them to rectify any error or omission in subsequent editions.

All facts are correct at the time of going to press.

Published 2013
Reprinted 2014

Text, design and layout © Rising Stars UK Ltd.

Authors: Les Ray and Gill Budgell

Educational consultant: Shareen Mayers, Routes to Success, Sutton

Text design: Green Desert Ltd

Cover design: West 8 Design

Illustrations: HL Studios

Publisher: Camilla Erskine

Copy Editor: Sarah Davies

British Library Cataloguing in Publication Data.
A CIP record for this book is available from the British Library.

ISBN: 978-0-85769-678-6

Printed by Craft Print International Ltd, Singapore